Phi

Moonfleece

Methuen Drama

Published by Methuen Drama 2010

1 3 5 7 9 10 8 6 4 2

Methuen Drama
A & C Black Publishers Limited
36 Soho Square
London W1D 3QY
www.methuendrama.com

ISBN 978 1 408 13055 1

A CIP catalogue record for this book is available from the British Library

Typeset by Mark Heslington Ltd, Scarborough, North Yorkshire
Printed and bound in Great Britain by CPI Cox & Wyman, Reading, Berkshire

Ben Monks and Will Young for

supporting
wall

Moonfleece

by Philip Ridley

Professional world premiere at Rich Mix, Bethnal Green Road, London, on Wednesday 3 March 2010.

Moonfleece

by Philip Ridley

Cast

in order of appearance

LINK	Reece Noi	SARAH	Emily Plumtree
GAVIN	Ashley George	NINA	Sian Robins-Grace
TOMMY	Bradley Taylor	ZAK	Beru Tessema
CURTIS	Sean Verey	WAYNE	Reeda Harris
ALEX	Krupa Pattani	STACEY	Alicia Davies
JEZ	David Ames		

Director	David Mercatali
Set and Lighting Design	William Reynolds
Costume Design	Ellan Parry
Sound Design	Ed Borgnis
Stage Manager	Heather Doole
Assistant Director & Workshop Co-Ordinator	Alice Lacey
Assistant Lighting Designer & Re-lighter	Christopher Nairne

Following performances at Rich Mix, the production toured to the Alhambra Studio Bradford, the Leicester Peepul Centre, the Birmingham Drum, the Doncaster Little Theatre, the Mill Theatre at the Dormston Centre Dudley, Riverside Studios London and the Greenwich Theatre.

www.supportingwall.com

Production supported by the Kobler Trust.

Ben Monks and Will Young supported by the Society of London Theatre and Theatre Management Association's Stage One Bursary for New Producers. For more information please visit *www.stageone.uk.com.*

Supporting Wall gratefully acknowledges the support of Deborah Hinton, Lord Archer and Mrs James.

Supporting Wall Ltd is a not for profit company registered in England and Wales, number 7081594.

Presented by kind permission of the Rod Hall Agency Limited of 6th Floor Fairgate House, 78 New Oxford Street, London WC1A 1HB.

THE COMPANY

Philip Ridley (Writer)

Philip was born in the East End of London where he still lives and works. He studied painting at St Martin's School of Art and his work has been exhibited widely throughout Europe and Japan. As well as three books for adults – and the highly acclaimed screenplay for the *The Krays* feature film (winner of The Evening Standard Best Film of the Year Award) – he has written seven adult stage plays: *The Pitchfork Disney*, the multi-award-winning *The Fastest Clock in the Universe, Ghost from a Perfect Place, Vincent River*, the highly controversial *Mercury Fur, Leaves of Glass* and *Piranha Heights*, plus several plays for young people: *Karamazoo, Fairytaleheart, Sparkleshark* and *Brokenville*.

He has also written many books for children, including *Scribbleboy* (shortlisted for the Carnegie Medal), *Kasper in the Glitter* (nominated for the Whitbread Prize), *Mighty Fizz Chilla* (shortlisted for the Blue Peter Book of the Year Award), *ZinderZunder, Vinegar Street, Zips'Apollo* and the bestseller *Krindlekrax* (winner of both the Smarties Prize and WH Smith's Mind-Boggling Books Award), the stage play of which – adapted by Philip himself – was premiered at the Birmingham Rep Theatre in the summer of 2002.

Philip has also directed three feature films from his own screenplays: *The Reflecting Skin* – winner of eleven international awards (including the prestigious George Sadoul Prize) – *The Passion of Darkly Noon* (winner of the Best Director Prize at the Porto Film Festival) and, most recently, *Heartless* (winner of The Silver Meliers Award for Best Fantasy Film), starring Jim Sturgess and Noel Clarke, due for release in May 2010. Last year saw the premiere of his first opera libretto, *Tarantula In Petrol Blue*, at Aldeburgh, with music by Anna Meredith. Philip has won both the Evening Standard's Most Promising Newcomer to British Film and Most Promising Playwright Awards – the only person ever to receive both prizes.

David Ames (Jez)

Theatre includes: *I Am Montana* (Arcola), *Love and Human Remains* (Croydon Warehouse), *Citizenship* (Jermyn Street), *Julius Caesar* (Barbican).

Television includes: *Doctor Who, Doctors, He Kills Coppers.*

Alicia Davies (Stacey)

Theatre includes: *La Cage aux Folles* (Playhouse, West End, and Menier Chocolate Factory), *Be My Baby* (Gatehouse Theatre), *Burning Cars* (Hampstead Theatre), *The Merchant of Venice, The Gondoliers* (Chichester Festival Theatre), *As you like it, Oh what a lovely war, Romeo and Juliet* (Regents Park Open Air Theatre), *Hard Times* (Theatre Royal Haymarket), *The Demon Headmaster* (National tour), *Les Misérables* (Palace Theatre London), *Fiddler on the Roof* (London Palladium).

Film includes: *Telstar.*

Television includes: *Holby City, Eastenders, From the Top.*

Ashley George (Gavin)

Trained at Webber Douglas.

Theatre includes: *Sing to Me Through Open Windows, Chains* (Orange Tree), *Deadlock* (national tour), *The Picture of Dorian Gray* (European Tour), *Measure for Measure* (Shakespeare's Globe), *Blue Remembered Hills* (Edinburgh Fringe), *Tooth of Crime* (Contact Theatre Manchester), *Skylight* (Stephen Joseph Theatre), *Equus, Romeo and Juliet, A Midsummer Night's Dream* (Rep Theatre Company).

Film includes: *Harry Brown, Firewood, No Hiding Place, Just the Ticket.*

Television includes: *Doctors, Holby City, The Bill, Wire in the Blood, Holmfirth Hollywood.*

Reeda Harris (Wayne)

Trained at Central School of Speech and Drama.

Theatre includes: *Christmas Cracker* (Southbank Centre), *A New World* (Shakespeare's Globe).

Reece Noi (Link)

Moonfleece is Reece's professional stage debut.

Film includes: *My Kingdom.*

Television includes: *Power of Poetry, Father and Son, Paradox, The Bill, Waterloo Road, Emmerdale, Doctors, Shameless, Grange Hill.*

Krupa Pattani (Alex)

Trained at Drama Studio London.

Theatre includes: *Dinnerladies* (No.1 tour), *Lichentongue* (Underbelly at Edinburgh Festival),*Unzipped* (Young Vic), *Starfish* (Y-Touring), *Unscripted* (Cockpit Theatre), *Handful of Henna* (The Crucible and UK Tour), *The Borrowers* (Midlands Arts Centre), *Child of the Divide* (Polka Theatre).

Television includes: *MI High, Casualty*

Radio includes: *Silver Street* (BBC)

Emily Plumtree (Sarah)

Emily graduated from the Central School of Speech and Drama in 2009. *Moonfleece* is her stage debut.

Television includes: *Hollyoaks Later.*

Sian Robins-Grace (Nina)

Theatre includes: *Love's Labours Lost* (Shakespeare's Globe and US tour), *A Midsummer Night's Dream* (Shakespeare's Globe), *Romeo and Juliet* (RSC), *Hamlet* (White Bear Theatre).

Bradley Taylor (Tommy)

Trained at the Drama Centre.

Theatre includes: *The Trepeaze Artist* (Tara Arts), *Some Trace of Her* (National), *Lilya* (Fink On Theatre), *Silverland* (Lacuna Theatre), *Doctor Faustus* (Bristol Old Vic).

Film includes: *Pumpkinhead IV: Blood Feud.*

Beru Tessema (Zak)

Trained at RADA.

Theatre includes: *King Lear, Troilus and Cressida, The Front Line* (Shakespeare's Globe), *Slaves* (Theatre 503) and *Hanjo* (Young Vic). Work for BBC radio includes: *Season of Migration to the North* and *Number One Ladies Detective Agency.*

Short films include: *Junction* and *Kismet.*

Sean Verey (Curtis)

Theatre includes: *Every Breath* (Y Touring), *A Christmas Carol* (Bristol Old Vic), *Through the Wire* (Tobacco Factory).

Film includes: *Dead Man Running, Bro, Jaws 1916.*

Television includes: *Skins Series 2, Casualty, Doctors, Holby City, The Bill, Half Moon Investigations, The Kindness of Strangers.*

David Mercatali (Director)

Directing includes: *People's Day* (Pleasance Theatre), *Zimpatch* (Oval House), *Weights, !Runners, Paint Over* (Blue Elephant Theatre), *!Runners – The Return* (Underbelly, Edinburgh Fringe), *Death of a Salesman* (Sherman Theatre, Cardiff).

Assistant Directing credits include: *Eleventh Capital* (Royal Court), *Funny Money* (British Theatre Playhouse, Singapore and Kuala Lumpur).

William Reynolds (Set and Lighting Design)

William trained at the Motley Theatre Design School.

Recent set and lighting designs include *Waiting* (Southbank Centre), *Mercury Fur* (Theatre Delicatessen), *Blood Wedding* (Southwark Playhouse), *La Boheme* (Palestinian Tour), *Just So* (Trafalgar Studios), *Saturday Night* (Arts Theatre and Theatre Royal Windsor) and *Jingo* (Finborough Theatre). Lighting designs – Daredevas (Southbank Centre), *Sniggle* (Theatre Royal Haymarket), *Nuit d'Electronique et d'Opera* (Theatre Royal de Wallonie, Belgium) and *The Magic Flute* (Palestinian Tour, Dir. Samuel West). Projection designs – *The Gambler* (Royal Opera House), *Das Rheingold* (National Reisopera, Holland) and *Home* (Theatre Royal Bath).

Ellan Parry (Costume Design)

Ellan trained at Wimbledon School of Art, and is a previous winner of the Jocelyn Herbert Award for Scenography and a Linbury Shortlisted Artist. Recent designs include *Carmen* (Blackheath Halls), *The Missionary's Position* (Penny Dreadful Productions), *As You Like It*, (Heartbreak Productions), *The Race* (Gecko), *Pot Noodle The Musical* (Mothervision), and stage visuals for indie-rock band Placebo's European tour. In the past year she has also worked as assistant designer on several major musicals, including John Doyle's *Oklahoma!* at Chichester Festival Theatre, and Trevor Nunn's Broadway transfer of *A Little Night Music.* Current projects include Katy Brand's *Big Ass Live Show*, and an Irish dance show in Poland, summer 2010, with her own company Release The Hounds.

Ed Borgnis (Sound Design)

Ed studied at Warwick University, before beginning his career at a film production company in Birmingham. Since going freelance, sound work for theatre includes the *Histories* cycle at the Camden Roundhouse, and seasons in Newcastle and London for the RSC, *Regent's Park Open Air* in 2008, *Far From The Madding Crowd* (English Touring Theatre), *The Picture of Dorian Gray* (European Arts) Tamasha's *Wuthering Heights, Last 5 Years* and *Tick Tick Boom* for *Notes from New York* (Duchess Theatre), *A Real Humane Person Who Cares and All That* (Arcola, directed by Jamie Harper for Rested Theatre). Ed has also tour and stage managed various comedy shows including *Frank Skinner's Credit Crunch Cabaret* and *Dave Gorman* on tour.

Heather Doole (Stage Manager)

Heather Doole is a Stage and Porduction Manager based in London.

Stage Management includes: *Medea* (Lazarus Theatre Company), *W.C. Fields – Lightly Boiled* (Top Edge Productions), *Hamlet Cut to the Bone* (Top Edge Productions), *Box of Tricks* (Parabox Magic).

Production Management includes: *Blood Wedding* (Metta Theatre), *Carnival of Wonders* (In the Gutter), *Duchess of Malfi* (Lazarus Theatre Company), *The Pirate, the Potato and the Camel and The Pirate the Potato and the Camel* (Top Edge Productions), *Brothers Lionheart* (Lionheart Productions).

Alice Lacey (Assistant Director and Workshop Co-Ordinator)

Directing includes: *Mercury Fur* (Hertford Bop Cellar), *Undermind* (Edinburgh Fringe), *Fantasia* (Old Vic 24 Hour Plays), *A Scene in a Kitchen* (Tristan Bates Theatre), *After the Flood* (Old Vic Symposium), *The Ostrich and the Dolphin* (Royal Institution and National Tour), *Greek Street and Sports* (Tristan Bates Theatre, Latitude Festival), *Macbeth* (Broadway Theatre).

Alice is director and curator of the Midnight Monologues, a series of site specific, one-on-one monologues (Tristan Bates Theatre, Latitude Festival) and Artistic Director of This Is Not A Play Area, a site-specific radio play project. In 2009, Alice was selected to take part in the Old Vic's 24 Hour Plays and Ignition at the Tristan Bates Theatre.

Christopher Nairne (Assistant Lighting Designer / Re-Lighter)

Recent and current lighting designs include: *La Bohème* (Cock Tavern Theatre), *Anyone Can Whistle* (Jermyn Street Theatre), *Henry V* (Southwark Playhouse), *Hedda* (Riverside Studios), *Generous* (Finborough Theatre), *Origin of the Species* (Arcola Theatre) and *Frisky and Mannish's School of Pop* (Sydney, Melbourne & UK tour). He has also worked extensively in Oxford and Edinburgh, as well as on two tours to Japan (*The Comedy of Errors* and *Love's Labour's Lost*). He previously assisted William Reynolds on *Cyrano de Bergerac* (Oxford Playhouse). Further details, and a full list of credits, are available on his website: *www.christophernairne.co.uk*.

Moonfleece

Characters

Link
Gavin
Tommy
Curtis
Alex
Jez
Sarah
Nina
Zak
Wayne
Stacey

A derelict flat on the top floor of a tower block in east London. The peeling wallpaper and decrepit furniture (small side table, armchair) indicate the place has not been 'officially' lived in for quite a while. There are, however, signs of more contemporary – if 'unofficial' – occupation: cans of lager, remains of fast food, a radio, a few books, sleeping bag, etc.

The boards covering the windows have been removed to reveal cracked, broken or missing glass (and afternoon sunlight). A few doors: to kitchen, balcony and the front door (broken off at hinges). A hallway in the flat leads, presumably, to bedrooms and bathroom.

A political banner can be seen. It has a family photo on it: smiling middle-aged couple, two teenaged sons and a teenaged girl (who, judging from the held hands and engagement rings, is the elder son's fiancée). They are all neatly dressed and very very smiling. Also, a pile of flyers, a box of badges (everything emblazoned with the cross of St George and 'VOTE AVALON') and a megaphone.

The sound of distant barking can be heard. This is loud to begin with but rapidly fades away.

Link *stands in the middle of the flat. He is fifteen years old and wearing scruffy jeans and trainers. His hair, like the rest of him, is in need of a wash.*

Link Who d'you fucking think you are? Eh? You can't just march in here and do what you bloody like. You don't own the fucking place.

Tommy *has come in from kitchen. He is eighteen years old and wearing a neat, light-grey suit. His hair, like the rest of him, is slick and tidy. He is muscular and tall for his age, a graceful giant at home with teacups and sledgehammers. He looks around the room as –*

Link You scared the bloody dogs. They can go on for hours like that, you know – Oi!

Tommy *has picked up a book.*

Slight pause.

Tommy *puts the book down.*

Gavin *enters from hallway. He is seventeen years old and, like* **Tommy**, *wearing a light-grey suit. Unlike* **Tommy**, *however, the effect is totally incongruous. Short, stocky and generally ungainly, he's like a Rottweiler in a tutu.*

Link I'm not here alone, you know. My mate – he lives here too. If he comes back and catches you – Fuck me! There'll be trouble. Big trouble. I can go and get him. Easy. I know where he is. He's down by the supermarket. If I screamed from the balcony – I bet he'd hear me.

Tommy *gets mobile phone from pocket.*

Gavin My turn to call!

Gets mobile from pocket.

. . . What'll I say?

Tommy Tell him we're in the flat.

Link My mate's older than me. He's strong. He looks after me. He can do things with his little finger you couldn't do with your . . . with a grenade-launching bazooka.

Gavin Voicemail.

Tommy Message.

Gavin Curtis. Gavin. Place secure. Awaiting further instructions. Over and out.

Link 'Over and out'? Who's he bloody think he is? The SAS?

Gavin Oi! Shut it!

Link Why should I?

Gavin Cos you value your kneecaps.

Tommy Gav!

Gavin It's *him*!

Points at **Link**.

Tommy (*to* **Link**) Listen. Why don't you make yourself scarce for an hour or so? Here's some money. Get yourself something to eat.

Link Stuff your money! This is *my* place.

Gavin Your *squat*!

Link I've still got rights!

Gavin You've got nothing!

Tommy Gavin!

Gavin You're an illegal immigrant, ain't you?

Link No.

Gavin What's your bloody name, then?

Link Ain't telling you!

Gavin Illegal! I can smell it on him.

Link Piss off!

Gavin What's your bloody name?

Link Rumpel-bloody-stiltskin.

Gavin Not English!

Tommy He's playing with you, for chrissakes.

Gavin Eh?

Tommy It's from a kids' story!

Gavin You bloody –

Makes a dash for **Link**.

Link *darts out of the way.*

Tommy Gavin! . . . Gav!

Holds **Gavin** *back.*

Link My mate'll kill you – you hurt me!

Tommy (*at* **Link**) No one's gonna hurt you.

Gavin No?

Tommy No! Stop it! . . . Stop!

Gavin . . . He's winding me up, Tommy.

Tommy You're winding yourself up! Okay? Now cool it . . . Cool it!

Gavin *calms down.*

Tommy *lets go of him.*

Slight pause.

Tommy Okay. Now . . . Let's all take a deep breath and start again, shall we?

Slight pause.

(*At* **Link**.) My name is Tommy. This is Gavin. What's yours?

Link *doesn't answer.*

Tommy Okay. Look . . . we're sorry we knocked down your door. That was very wrong of us. Wasn't it, Gav?

Silence.

Okay. We knocked it down because we were unaware anyone was living here.

Link You could've bloody knocked.

Gavin It's a derelict bloody tower block, you foreign bloody bastard.

Tommy All right! I accept – *we* accept – we should've knocked. We're sorry. We weren't thinking. Were we, Gavin?

Gavin *doesn't answer.*

Tommy Okay. Me and Gavin – we've been very busy lately, you see, and sometimes . . . well, sometimes we get a bit carried away . . . we didn't mean any harm . . . honestly . . .

Link *is looking at banners etc.*

Gavin Don't touch those.

Tommy He can touch them for chrissakes! – We're campaigning. There's an election next week.

Link I know that. Not stupid.

Gavin No?

Link No! . . . Tell me, why ain't you put your *real* symbol on this lot?

Gavin (*at* **Tommy**) What's he mean?

Link You see, if you'd put your *real* symbol on all this then I would have understood. I mean . . . I would have known exactly who I was dealing with. All your huffing and your puffing and your blowing my door down.

Gavin He's a bloody retard.

Tommy Gav!

Link Tattoos! You must have had it tattooed on you somewhere.

Gavin You're winding me up again.

Tommy No, he's not – Tattoo?

Link Yeah. Come on! Show me!

Tommy I don't understand what you –

Link Your swastikas!

Gavin It's prejudiced comments like that get your foreign fucking head kicked in!

Tommy Gav!

Gavin He's ignorant.

Tommy Well, we ain't gonna educate him by shouting.

Link I don't need educating about you lot.

Tommy We are an official political party.

Gavin We take old people on day trips to Southend.

Link *White* old people!

Gavin Pakis don't like the seaside.

Tommy Gav! Jesus! Remember what Mr Avalon says. 'Don't heckle a heckler. Educate through – ' Gav? What does Mr Avalon say? Educate through . . . ?

Gavin . . . Reasonable debate.

Link Oh! You can *reasonably* debate, can you?

Gavin Yes!

Link This I *must* see! Go on. Debate. Reasonably.

Slight pause.

Tommy Go on, Gav.

Link Go on, Gav.

Gavin . . . Good evening, ladies and gentlemen.

Link It's afternoon.

Tommy Think before you speak, Gav.

Link Ooo, getting tricky, eh, Gav?

Gavin . . . Good afternoon, ladies and gentleman – Gentlemen! I want to thank you all for coming out on such a chilly night. Warm day –

Points at **Link**.

(*At* **Tommy**) He's laughing at me!

Tommy Perhaps you should skip to the introduction bit . . . 'I'd like to introduce you to –'

Gavin I know, I know!

Indicates photo on banner.

I'd like to introduce you to a family. They've been an important family in my life and hopefully they'll become an important family in yours. This is Mr Avalon. You might have seen him around. He's lived in East London all his life. His dad lived here before him. Mr Avalon can trace his family roots back to William the Conqueror.

Link Who was French.

Gavin Says who?

Tommy Just . . . just carry on.

Gavin This is Mrs Avalon. She's lived here all her life too. East London born and bred. She's the perfect mum and wife is Mrs Avalon. No one cooks roast beef like her. This is their eldest son. His name's Wayne. And this is Wayne's fiancée, the beautiful Stacey. They got engaged when they were sixteen. Childhood sweethearts. Next year, when Wayne's twenty-two, they're gonna get married. It's gonna be the biggest bash east London's seen in years. Who knows? If you're a friend of the family – like me – you might get an invitation too.

Link Bet it's gonna be a really white wedding, eh?

Tommy Why don't you give him a chance?

Gavin This is Curtis! Curtis is the youngest son! He's eighteen. He's left school now and is working in his dad's double-glazing business down Mile End Road. Curtis is a bit of a thinker. He's got a shelf full of books in his room –

Link *yawns and walks away.*

Gavin Oi!

Grabs megaphone and yells through it –

We don't believe in public floggings here.

Tommy That's right!

Gavin We don't believe in cutting hands off here. We don't believe in honour killings here.

Tommy What *do* we believe in?

Gavin We believe in the history and tradition of this great nation. Our aim is to give this nation back its self-respect. To do that we've got to rediscover the spirit and values that made us rule the waves.

Tommy Go for it, mate!

Gavin The family!

Tommy Yes!

Gavin Moral values.

Tommy Christian values.

Gavin For this is a Christian country.

Tommy Always has been.

Gavin Royalty! Tradition!

Tommy Work ethic!

Gavin Respect for the law!

Tommy Neighbour helping neighbour.

Gavin A clean doorstep!

Tommy The Blitz spirit reborn!

Gavin This is the future I see.

Tommy Who can give us this future?

Gavin (*chanting with* **Tommy**) Avalon . . . Avalon . . . Avalon . . .

Tommy (*chanting with* **Gavin**) Avalon . . . Avalon . . . Avalon . . .

Distant dogs, disturbed by the noise, start barking as –

Curtis *arrives in doorway, holding a torch. He is eighteen years old and wearing a light grey suit that fits him to perfection. He is fair-haired, glossily good-looking, as slick and smooth as a shark in baby oil. He watches as –*

Gavin (*chanting with* **Tommy**) Avalon . . .

Tommy (*chanting with* **Gavin**) Ava—

Gavin *and* **Tommy** *see* **Curtis**.

Tommy Oh . . . Hello, Curtis.

Gavin Hello, Curtis.

Curtis Your racket set the dogs off.

Tommy Sorry, mate. We . . . er . . . we got a little carried away.

The noise of the dogs starts to fade.

Gavin I've been educating someone, Curtis.

Indicates **Link**.

Gavin I've been giving him the full Gav treatment.

Link It worked! I'm a convert! – Sieg Heil, Curtis!

Gives Nazi salute.

Gavin Oi! Respect! – And keep your distance!

Stands between **Curtis** *and* **Link**.

Curtis (*indicating* **Link**) Tommy?

Tommy Says he lives here. Two of them apparently. Other one's out somewhere.

Gavin Begging probably.

Link He's a street entertainer.

Gavin Exactly! – You get my message, Curt? I left a message with an update. Did you get it?

Curtis No.

Tommy I've informed this individual we'll only be requiring the premises for a short period but he still refuses to vacate.

Curtis I'm sure he'll go if you ask him nicely – Won't you?

Link Bollocks!

Gavin Oi! Don't forget who you're talking to.

Link I ain't! Bollocks! Know what you lot did? In the last place I lived? Went around throwing severed pigs' heads into mosques. Their idea of fun. You should hang your head in shame. All of you. You're nothing but scum! Scum!

Curtis . . . I'll deal with you later.

Link Ooo, you're turning me on!

Gavin Don't be disgusting!

Link *Me* disgusting!?

Curtis *starts looking round the flat.*

Link So . . . what's your story, eh? You lot? Wanna use this place for a secret HQ or something? Print hate mail? Make petrol bombs?

Curtis Where's the table and stuff, Tom?

Tommy What table and stuff?

Curtis The fold-up table. The one from the back of the meeting hall. And chairs. They're supposed to be here.

Tommy First I've heard.

Curtis *stares at* **Gavin**.

Tommy *follows the stare.*

Tommy Bloody hell, Gav.

Gavin I put everything in the back of the car.

Curtis So where's the car?

Gavin Down by the museum.

Curtis Well, it ain't doing much good there, is it?

Gavin It's him!

Points at **Tommy**.

Tommy Me?

Gavin We were in the car, Curtis. I was giving it the ol' 'Vote Avalon' business out the window. Going great guns, I was. We had some time to spare. *He* suggested we park the car and walk through Bethnal Green Road market. There I was! 'Vote Avalon'. Flyers! Badges. We got all the way down to the supermarket. We stood outside for a while. Twenty people told me we had their vote in all, Curtis. Twenty! Not bad, eh?

Curtis Cut to the chase!

Gavin *He* said it wasn't worth going back for the car.

Pointing at **Tommy**.

Tommy I didn't know there was stuff in the boot we needed, did I?

Gavin You didn't bloody ask!

Tommy Gimme strength!

Curtis Jesus, don't tell me you walked up those stairs without a torch.

Gavin *gets lighter from pocket and lights it.*

Gavin I lit the way with this, Curt!

Curtis You said you'd quit smoking.

Gavin . . . I'm trying!

Curtis No ciggies. No drink. No nothing. We've got to be squeaky clean. You know that.

Gavin Sorry.

Tommy Want me to go back for them?

Curtis Eh? What?

Tommy The chairs and table.

Curtis There's no time now. It's gonna kick off any minute.

Link What's gonna 'kick off'?

Gavin Your head if you don't fuck off!

Curtis Gavin! Jesus! . . . A word, mate – Come here.

Slight pause.

Gavin *goes over to* **Curtis**.

Curtis If you use any more language like that I will be forced to tell Dad and –

Gavin But, Curt –

Curtis No, no, listen, mate, listen. You've been warned before.

Gavin . . . I know.

Curtis *What* were you warned? Tell me.

Gavin No . . . no bad language.

Curtis No bad language. And no threatening language. Wayne won't come to your rescue every time.

Gavin The party's everything to me.

Curtis I know that, mate. Now, put your thinking cap on and let's solve the table and chairs situation. Can you do that for me?

Gavin Sure thing, Curt.

Looks at **Tommy**, *then indicates* **Link**.

Curtis Give him some money.

Link Stuff your money. This is *my* place!

Curtis No. It's not.

Gavin What about this?

Points at small side table.

Curtis It's . . . not quite big enough, mate. We need to sit around it.

Gavin Armchair?

Curtis No.

Gavin Two people can sit on the arms and –

Curtis No! We need a proper table with proper chairs like I told you to bloody – Jesus! Tommy?

Tommy We'll check the other flats. Might strike lucky. How many chairs?

Curtis Three.

Tommy No worries – Oi! Mr Memory!

Tommy *and* **Gavin** *leave.*

Link *is looking at the Avalon family photo on the banner.*

Link So . . . what's it like having your family photo used as a piece of political propaganda?

Curtis . . . It's fine.

Link This your garden?

Curtis Eh?

Link Where the photo was taken.

Curtis Yes.

Link The roses look . . . a bit odd.

Curtis They were put in afterwards.

Link What?

Curtis Computer. The roses were sort of . . . pasted on or something. I dunno. That's Wayne's department.

Link Your brother?

Curtis My *step*brother.

Sound of distant door being kicked in.

Dogs start barking.

Link Your mate's turned door-kicking into an art form.

Curtis He's a trained athlete.

Link Crowbars're easier. You just get it under the lock and – Krack! Open says-a-me.

Curtis The crowbar and other useful items are in the car. As you heard.

Link Your mates – they ain't the sharpest tools in the tool shed, are they?

Curtis Oi! Tommy's all right!

Has been dialling on his mobile phone and now –

Hi . . . I'm in the flat . . . Yeah, yeah, odd. Very odd . . . How far away are you? . . . I thought you might be here by now . . . Thought you said you finished at four on Saturdays . . . Oh, right . . . Look, forget buses, Sarah. Call a minicab. I'll pay . . . Sarah, we can't run late. It's gonna get dark and there's no lighting here, you know . . . Okay, okay . . . Call up when you arrive and I'll send Tom down with the money . . . Good . . . And Sarah? Thanks.

Hangs up.

Link So . . . who's Sarah?

Sound of dogs has faded now.

Curtis *looks round flat.*

Link Girlfriend?

No answer.

You *want* her as a girlfriend?

No answer.

Ex-girlfriend!

Curtis Shut it!

Another door kicked in.

Dogs bark.

Link So . . . why's ex-girlfriend Sarah coming here?

Curtis What's it to you?

Link I have a natural curiosity in every fascist who occupies my home!

Curtis It's *my* home!

Link Of course. *Everything* belongs to you lot, don't it?

Curtis No. Not everything. But *this* flat – You see that armchair? There was another one like that. Here. A sofa – here! There? Telly! There was a big mirror up here. Photos on the mantelpiece. Ornaments. A snow globe. And in the bedroom at the end of the corridor – In the end room? Are there . . . paintings on the wall?

Link Yeah. Fairy-tale stuff.

Curtis God. Still there.

Rushes for bedroom, then hesitates.

Link Go on! . . . What's stopping you?

Curtis . . . Nothing.

Link Did you paint them?

Curtis No. My brother did.

Link My mate thinks they're amazing. He loves fairy tales. We've got a book with them in. See? We look at one a night. He's teaching me to read. He's a great teacher. When he tells a story . . . everything else – all my problems – they all just float away. It's like you're *in* the story. You know?

Curtis . . . Yeah.

Link Zak tells stories on the street. That's my mate. Zak. I help him sometimes. I'm the official Storyteller Apprentice. I say, 'Ladies and gentleman! Roll up, roll up. Spare us a few minutes of your time and enter a world of enchantment and wonder. We bring you stories! Fantasy. Thriller.

Thriller-fantasy. Comedy-weepie-fantasy! Zak here will spin a tale of surprise and magic before your very eyes. Nothing is prepared. Just call out three things and Zak will spin a web of a story to take your breath away.'

Curtis And does he?

Link Yeah. Always. Most people clear off. Some stay to hear the whole thing, though. I go round and collect money.

Slight pause.

Tell you one thing. Your brother's better at painting than photo whatsit.

Curtis Eh – ?

Link These pasted-on roses.

Curtis Oh, that's not *him*, for chrissakes. That's Wayne. I told you. My *step*brother.

Link So . . . who did the paintings in the bedroom?

Curtis Jason. My *real* brother.

Link So . . . who's your step-parent? Mum or dad?

Curtis . . . No more questions.

Link Why not? I ain't going anywhere. I'm naturally inquisitive. Zak says I'm the chattiest chatterbox he's ever met. Gets me in trouble sometimes.

Curtis It's getting you in trouble now.

Link I just wanna know who your step-parent is. What's the big deal? I bet it's your mum.

Curtis No.

Link Gotcha!

Another door.

More dogs.

Slight pause.

Link So . . . what's up with Jason, then?

Curtis What?

Link No real brother Jason with real mummy in propaganda family photo.

Curtis You've got three seconds to disappear.

Link Or what?

Curtis One!

Link Real brother Jason disagree with the step-family politics, eh?

Curtis Two.

Link *doesn't move.*

Slight pause.

Link Two and a half?

Curtis What's wrong with you?

Link What's wrong with *me*?

Curtis All I'm asking you to do is give me some . . . some time here . . .

Link This is *my* place!

Curtis Jesus Christ, ain't you heard *anything* I've said, you bloody stupid – ? Listen! My gran was the first person to move into this tower block. They were still laying cement. If you go to the basement there's handprints in the floor. My gran's. My mum – she was born in this flat. She had her wedding reception in this flat. My mum and dad lived in this flat. My first dad. My *real* dad. When Gran died she was buried from this flat. The big bedroom down the hall? That's where Jason was born. Me too. The four of us lived here and we were bloody happy. Mum, Dad, Jason and me. Everyone respected Mum and Dad. They came to them for advice and stuff. If anyone had a complaint against a neighbour they didn't go to the council or anything. They went to Mum. They went to Dad. *They* sorted it out. Always. When Dad died – I tell you, the whole bloody block stood outside to pay their respects. And the flowers! The car park was covered. You could smell 'em right down to the supermarket. Local papers took photographs. We had drinks and sandwiches in here afterwards. Neighbours queued up for hours – hours! – to pay their respects. You see this armchair? Mum sat here and cried so much the cushions were wet for weeks. Months. Dad's death ripped her to bloody pieces. You ever seen that happen to someone you love? Eh? It's shit! I'd rather kill myself than see that again! My brother – Jason, my *real* brother – he had to look after me. He was seven years older. He washed my clothes and got me to school and . . . and cooked my dinner and . . . – Don't you *dare* refer to this flat as yours! Hear me? Don't *dare*! It'll *never* be yours. It'll never be anyone's except mine. Even when they dynamite the place – and it's nothing but rubble – the rubble that makes up this flat will have my name running through it!

Alex (*off, calling*) Sarah?

Link Who's that?

Alex Sarah?

Curtis Jesus . . .

Alex *strides in, holding torch. She is eighteen years old and wearing combat trousers, T-shirt and denim jacket. Her hair is short and tousled. Confident and swaggering, she seems to be constantly on the precipice of an argument and relishing the prospect of jumping in head first.*

Alex Blimey, what's this? The fascist version of Halloween. Dress up like a respectable person.

Curtis What you doing here?

Alex Sarah not turned up yet?

Curtis Alex!?

Alex I'm here for Sarah!

Curtis Did she *ask* you to come?

Alex I'm surprising her.

Curtis Why're you always sticking your big bloody nose in?

Alex Let's think. Perhaps it's like ... Yeah! Like when I'm watching *Sleeping Beauty*. The bit where the Princess is using the spinning wheel. You know? The wicked whatever has put poison on the prick of the needle. Every time I watch that scene I can't help sticking my big bloody nose in and calling out, 'Don't go near the poisoned prick!'

Link *laughs.*

Alex Oh, hello, mate – Hang on! Don't tell me! You live here, right?

Link They kicked my door in.

Alex (*at* **Curtis**) Pig!

Holds hand out to **Link**.

Alex Alex.

Link Link.

Alex Oh?

Link When I was a kid I kept running away.

Alex The missing Link! I like it.

Link Yeah, me too.

Alex You and me'll stick together, Link. We'll be the underground freedom fighters against the Imperial Storm Troopers.

Curtis What did Sarah tell you?

Alex About?

Curtis This!

Alex Everything.

Curtis Jesus! She promised she wouldn't tell anyone.

Alex I am not *anyone*, pal.

Link What they doing here, Alex?

Curtis Not a word.

Alex Hitler Youth's seen a ghost.

Link A ghost!

Gavin *and* **Tommy** *can be heard struggling in with the table.*

Alex Oh, no. Don't tell me. Not all three Ugly Sisters in one room. This is too good to be true.

Gavin *and* **Tommy** *appear with table.*

Alex Hello, ladies.

Gavin What's she doing here?

Curtis Nothing to do with me.

Tommy You're not welcome, Alex.

Alex From you, that's a compliment.

Link What ghost you been seeing?

Curtis Shut it!

Alex Pig!

Gavin *and* **Tommy** *are having trouble with the table.*

Tommy Careful!

Gavin It's you!

Jez (*calling, off*) Al-lex?

Curtis Jesus! Who's that?

Alex Jez! – You all right, babes?

Jez Where are you, babes?

Alex Walk straight the corridor.

Jez I'm getting lost.

Alex Hang on, babes.

Tries to get past **Gavin** *and* **Tommy**.

Curtis Who the hell's this Jez?

Alex You bringing that table in, boys, or is this some sexual fetish of yours?

Gavin Don't be disgusting!

Curtis Alex! Who's this Jez?

Alex A mate!

Goes to grab table.

Gavin Hands off our table!

Alex *Your* table.

Link They own *everything*!

Curtis This ain't some bloody free-for-all, you know. I don't want the whole world and his bloody cousin to – Jesus!

Starts dialling on mobile.

Alex Phoning Sarah? Go ahead! What d'you think she's gonna say? 'Ooo, tell that pesky Alex to clear off, Curt baby'? You arrogant pig! I'm surprised she's agreed to come here at all after what you did.

Tommy What did *he* do?

Alex You can't be serious?

Curtis *Sarah* stopped talking to *me*!

Tommy That's right!

Curtis No reason!

Alex No *reason*? You want the full essay or just the bullet points? You lied! You're full of hate! You preach hate! Your views stink! You're a pig! You'll breed pigs! Want me to carry on? You took that precious thing – the most precious thing in the whole world – and you shat on it from a great height. 'Oh, you should see us when we're alone, Al. He's so affectionate. I look into his big eyes and – ' Big eyes. The wolf had big eyes! And teeth! The teeth you lied through, you heartless piece of – What was it you said to her? 'Oh, I'm not really part of all this Avalon stuff, Sarah. I'm not political. I just go along with it cos I don't wanna upset Mum.' Then what happens? A little secretive Easter rally in the middle of Epping Forest. A family day out with smiley grannies and toddlers chanting, 'England for the white!' I was standing next to her when she heard you speak. Her world fell apart.

Curtis She would never've known about it if it weren't for you.

Alex I had a *duty* to tell her.

Curtis A *duty*!?

Alex Yes! As her friend. To show her what you really are.

Tommy What you did broke Sarah's heart.

Curtis *I'd* never treat a friend like that.

Tommy Nor me.

Alex I can't . . . I can't believe what I'm bloody hearing – Jesus! Listen to me, you pair of delusional pricks. It wasn't me who broke her to pieces! It was me who picked up the pieces. It was me who held her when she cried. She was on medication for months. You know that? Course you don't! Not even a bloody phone call.

Link You could've bloody phoned.

Curtis I *did* phone.

Tommy Sarah wouldn't speak to him.

Alex Not even a card when she jumped in the canal and tried to . . . Oh, shit! Shit!

Curtis Jumped? . . . Alex?

Alex . . . Forget it.

Curtis I heard . . . I was *told* she slipped and fell into the canal. An accident . . . Tom?

Tommy That's what I was told.

Gavin Me too.

Alex It's what *everyone* was told! Okay? It's what her family wanted. Sarah got a little drunk one night and slipped into the canal. Her friends – me included – had to fish her out. Everyone was giggling. All a bit of a laugh. But it wasn't a bloody laugh. Far from it. Now you know.

Jez (*calling, off*) Alex?

Alex Yes!

Alex *strides over to table and effortlessly lifts it high.*

She plonks it down and leaves.

Pause.

Tommy . . . Okay. Let's get the table in place, shall we?

Curtis Tom . . . Sarah tried to . . .

Tommy We can't think of that now, mate.

Curtis You *swear* you didn't know.

Tommy I'd never lie to you, mate. You know that.

Curtis Yeah, mate. I know.

Gavin Oi! Lovebirds! Where's the table going?

Tommy Well, let's see . . .

Gavin *and* **Tommy** *pick up table.*

Tommy About here, Curt?

Slight pause.

Curt?

Curtis What? Oh, yeah, fine.

Tommy *and* **Gavin** *put table in place.*

Curtis'*s mobile rings.*

He checks it.

Curtis ... Tom?

Tommy Sarah?

Curtis *nods.*

The mobile continues ringing.

Tommy You gonna answer it, mate?

Slight pause.

Curtis *hands mobile out to* **Tommy**.

Tommy *takes mobile and answers it.*

Tommy (*into mobile*) Hi, Sarah, it's Tom ... Okay, right down.

Gives phone back to **Curtis**.

Tommy Everything's all right, mate. Don't worry.

Slight pause.

Come here. Relax.

Rubs **Curtis**'*s shoulders.*

Curtis There's no time for that, mate.

Tommy No one wins a fight when they're tense.

Gavin I'm tense.

Tommy That's how you're meant to bloody be!

Continues to rub **Curtis**'*s shoulders.*

Tommy You're all knots and tangles ... There ... Better?

Curtis Thanks, Tom.

Tommy (*at* **Gavin**) Come on, Mr Tense!

Tommy *rushes out followed by* **Gavin**.

Slight pause.

Link So . . . was it someone you knew?

Curtis Eh? Who?

Link The ghost.

Curtis Yeah, yeah, someone I knew.

Link Your *real* dad?

Curtis No.

Link Then who?

Curtis I . . . I don't wanna talk about it. Please.

Link I saw a ghost once. The last foster place I was in. A kid from years ago. Said he'd been chopped up and buried in the cellar. Foster couple looked so kind and cosy. But you never can tell. The bloke collected beer mats so something weren't right. I'd like to collect seashells but I've got nowhere to keep them. Do you collect anything?

Curtis Do I – ? Look! Don't take this the wrong way but I'm not really in the mood to shoot the breeze about – oh, Christ! The taxi money! Tommy! Tom!

Rushes out as **Alex** *and* **Jez** *come in.*

They collide.

Alex Don't let us get in your way, will you! Pig!

Curtis *has gone, calling after* **Tommy**.

Jez *is seventeen years old. His clothes are stylish and casual. Like* **Alex**, *there is something brave and fearless about him. He is carrying a small bag and a torch.*

Link Sarah's downstairs.

Alex Oh, Jez!

Rushes to balcony.

Jez Look at this place! Am I Aladdin in the cave or what? – Oh! Link, I presume.

Link Us three against the Imperial Storm Troopers, eh?

Jez You bet, babes.

Talks into microphone.

I am talking to Link who is the current occupant of 127 Sunrise Heights – now commonly known as Wild Dog Heights – the top-floor flat where Curtis Avalon was born. Tell me, Link, how long have you been here?

Link Er . . . almost a week.

Jez And what is your first impression of Curtis?

Link He's a pig.

Jez Agreed. But do you think he's a *sexy* pig?

Link What?

Alex *has come back in looking a little shell-shocked.*

Jez Babes? What's up?

Alex She's wearing the new dress.

Jez Not the one you bought her?

Alex It was an anniversary present, Jez. Two years of wonderful friendship. And now she wears it to . . . to . . .

Link Perhaps it was the only clean dress she had.

Jez Exactly. Thank you, Link – Babes! You gonna let the fascists see you upset? Eh? . . . Eh?

Alex Who's upset? Me? Ha!

Jez That's my babes.

Link What's all this for?

Indicates tape recorder.

Jez What – ? Oh, I'm doing a – how shall I say – a study of Curtis.

Link Why?

Jez I want to get into his mind.

Alex Into his pants more like.

Jez My, someone ate a big bowl of wisecracks for breakfast.

Link How can you fancy that fascist?

Jez 'I Was A Teenage Fascist Fancier.' How's that for a title?

Alex Jez has a theory about Curtis.

Jez About why he became a fascist. And it's not a theory! It's fact!

Link What is it?

Jez Guilt!

Link About what?

Jez The state his mum got in after his dad – his *real* dad – was killed.

Link Curtis's real dad was . . . *killed*!?

Alex Murdered.

Link What happened?

Alex Oh, you don't want to hear all the –

Jez Gruesome details? Course he does.

Link Course I do.

Alex Well, you tell him, then.

Jez No. Curtis told Sarah and Sarah told you. So you're nearest to the source as they say in journalist circles. Besides, I haven't heard you tell it since I got this.

Indicates tape recorder.

(*Into microphone.*) The story of the fateful night of Curtis's *real* daddy's death as told by Alex Pattani while sitting in the very flat where the deceased man lived and died. Wow! – Alex?

Alex Curtis's dad went down to the supermarket and –

Jez Set the scene. Come on, babes. Snow.

Slight pause.

Alex It was snowing. Winter.

Jez December.

Alex Curtis wasn't very well.

Jez Nor was his brother.

Link Jason.

Jez Who told you about Jason?

Link Curtis.

Jez Lordy, he must really like you. What's your secret?

Link I just ask a lot of questions.

Alex Curtis and Jason had been out playing in the snow.

Jez Victoria Park. The lake was frozen.

Alex The brothers caught a chill or something. Although, from what Sarah says, Curtis was a sickly child generally.

Jez Hard to believe when you see him now.

Alex Oh, perr-leease.

Link The murder!

Alex Curtis's mum asked Dad to go down to the chemist and get one of those lemon-powder things.

Link To make a lemon drink?

Alex Exactly. So Dad walks down to the supermarket and gets the lemon powder and –

Jez A bit more 'oomph', babes.

Alex 'Oomph'?

Link Jez is right. You need to create the pictures a bit more. *Feel* it.

Jez Exactly

Link If you feel it, then *we* will feel it. And we'll follow you anywhere.

Slight pause.

Alex It's a blizzard. Howling wind! Icicles on every windowsill.

Link The very concrete is shivering.

Jez Oh, I like that.

Alex Who's that man making his way across the car park?

Link It's Curtis's dad!

Alex He looks so cold. His fingers are blue with cold.

Link But his two sons are sick.

Jez They need their lemon drink.

Alex Muggers!

Link No!

Jez They jump out of the dark.

Alex They're hitting and kicking Curtis's dad.

Link They want his money.

Alex Dad won't give it to them. They struggle. Dad falls to the ground. The muggers run off.

Link Did they get away with anything?

Alex His wallet.

Jez And wristwatch.

Alex Dad picks the medicine up from the snow.

Jez He starts to walk home.

Link Is he hurt?

Alex He's dripping with blood.

Jez He leaves a trail behind him.

Link Like a trail of breadcrumbs.

Jez Blood-red breadcrumbs!

Link Like rose petals.

Jez Oh, yesss!

Link A trail of rose petals in the snow.

Jez Oh, yesss!

Alex . . . You two finished?

Jez and **Link** Sorry.

Alex Dad gets back to the tower block. The lifts ain't working. He walks up the stairs.

Jez All twenty-one floors.

Link A rose petal of blood on every step.

Alex Stop it! . . . Dad opens the front door to the flat. Dad walks down the hall. Dad walks into the room and –

Curtis *steps into room.*

Slight pause.

Curtis Don't stop on my account.

Alex Curtis's real dad is covered in blood. Mum screams. Jason screams. Curtis screams. And Curtis's real Dad falls dead. There! Right in front of his whole family.

Curtis Almost. He died in hospital the next day. He'd been stabbed seven times.

Link I'm sorry.

Jez Were you with him when he died?

Curtis Yes.

Jez What were his last words?

Curtis He asked me if I was feeling better ... Anything else?

Link Were they caught?

Curtis The killers? Course not. Black faces into the black night.

Alex Or white faces into the white snow.

Curtis Dad knew the difference between black and white.

Sees **Jez** *holding microphone towards him.*

Curtis Hang on! What's all this?

Link He's studying you.

Alex It's for the magazine.

Jez *R.Y.A.P. Monthly.*

Alex *Rainbow Youth Against Prejudice.*

Jez We meet at the library.

Alex Every Thursday evening.

Jez You're more than welcome to join.

Curtis Gimme that!

Grabs for tape recorder.

Jez Fuck off!

Curtis You've got no right to be here.

Jez On the contrary, mein Führer. I have every right. This tower block is now a public space. Ergo, whatever happens here is, in journalist terms, up for grabs so – to coin a phrase – tough bloody titties.

Has taken a camera from his bag and now takes a photo of **Curtis** *– Flash!*

Curtis Stop that.

Jez Public space.

Flash!

Curtis That's it! The whole thing's off.

Alex What?

Curtis You heard!

Dials phone.

Jez *takes photo – Flash!*

Curtis I'm warning you!

Jez He's *so* sexy when he's angry.

Takes another photo.

Curtis *faces wall, his back to front door.*

Curtis (*into mobile*) I'm calling it off . . . Well, Tommy's told you who's here, I suppose . . . Yes! But she's brought this Jez pillock.

Alex Jez pillock?

Jez Sounds like a detergent.

Curtis No, Sarah, he's taking photos and stuff.

Jez 'Buy Jezpillock for those stubborn fascist stains.'

Curtis This is supposed to be private, Sarah! Me, you, Tommy – No! Go back downstairs. I'm sorry for the trouble. I was stupid to go ahead with something like this in the first place. I must have been mad or something.

Sarah *has appeared, holding mobile to ear. She is seventeen years old and wearing a simple and stylish dress. She's obviously had her hair done and her make-up is slight but very effective. She is carrying a bag.*

Alex *and* **Jez** *watch, expectant.*

Curtis Sarah? You there? Can you hear me?

Sarah Yes.

Curtis *freezes.*

Pause.

Sarah Hello, Curtis.

Curtis *keeps his back to her.*

Curtis . . . Hello.

Slight pause.

Sarah You gonna look at me?

Curtis Yeah. Course I am.

Slowly – oh-so-slowly – **Curtis** *turns.*

Pause.

Sarah This place . . . everything looks so small.

Curtis Yeah.

Sarah I remember it being . . . you know.

Curtis Yeah.

Jez *takes photo – Flash!*

Curtis There! *That's* what I'm talking about!

Sarah Hello, you two.

Jez Couldn't let beauty go to the beast's castle alone, could we?

Alex Especially in a dress like that.

Sarah I wore it for work, Al. We had the chief librarian round this afternoon. Official visit. I had to look my best. So . . . I wore my best.

Alex And that's the *only* reason?

Sarah The *only* reason.

Link I'm Link.

Sarah Hello.

Nina (*off, calling*) Sarah! Coo-eee! Sar-rah?

Sarah Nina! – You okay, Neen?

Gavin *and* **Tommy** *appear, carrying* **Nina** *in a wheelchair. She is twenty years old and wearing a bright green dress and lots of jewellery (mostly green and blue glass). Her hair has been tinted to suit her generally aquamarine appearance.*

Nina Careful! Stop jolting me! Talk about a life on the ocean waves.

Tommy Stop rocking her, Gav!

Gavin It's you!

Alex Out the way.

Nudges **Gavin** *aside.*

Nina Hello, my dear.

Alex Hello, gorgeous.

Nina They give me the giant from the beanstalk on this side and . . . one of the seven dwarfs on the other.

Link Dopey.

Link, **Alex**, **Jez** *and* **Nina** *laugh.*

Gavin Shut up! – (*At* **Curtis** *and* **Tommy**.) Why don't you stick up for me?

Alex *and* **Tommy** *bring* **Nina** *into room and put her down.*

Tommy Careful.

Alex No? Really?

Nina Those stairs are truly an adventure! You see the dog crap on the fourth floor? It was sculptural, my dears, sculptural – Afternoon to you, Jez.

Jez Afternoon, sexy.

Tommy One of your wheels look a bit wonky.

Nina I slipped down the kerb this morning.

Tommy It just needs a – Hang on!

Pushes wheel into place.

Nina Oh, my!

Tommy That should do it!

Link The Wheelchair Chiropractor.

Jez That could be a telly series.

Link 'Whose wonky wheel will he fix this week?'

Jez I'm hooked already.

Nina What aftershave you wearing, young man?

Tommy I . . . I dunno. It was a present.

Curtis Ocean Spray.

Nina Ocean Spray! May I have another whiff?

Tommy *leans forward.*

Nina Mmmm.

Tommy *stands upright.*

Tommy You . . . you want us to hunt out some chairs now, Curt?

Alex Don't bother.

Jez It's off, apparently.

Nina Off?

Tommy Why?

Curtis This one's taking liberties.

Indicates **Jez***.*

Gavin Tell him to piss off.

Tommy Gavin's right.

Alex He goes, I go.

Sarah She goes, I go.

Nina She goes, I go.

Curtis Well. There you have it. Sarah, thanks for asking Nina to help. It's a shame certain friends of yours couldn't keep their bloody noses out of things that don't bloody concern them. And it's an even a bigger shame, now that they *are* here, you won't tell them to go. Nina, thanks for agreeing to help – Tom?

Heads for door.

Nina Ahhhh! There's something here ... I feel it ... Secrets!

Curtis *stops.*

Nina Terrible secrets ... Suffocating secrets – Sarah, where's my refreshing libation? Quick! Quick!

Sarah *gets a bottle from the bag she's carrying and gives it to* **Nina**.

Nina *drinks.*

Sarah She's susceptible to atmospheres.

Nina When I was a child I heard voices. 'Nina,' they said, 'one day you'll be a ballet dancer.' What a sense of humour the spirit world has, eh?

Gavin That's gin!

Points at **Nina**'*s bottle.*

Nina Slander! I'm a respectable children's librarian!

Gavin I can smell it from here.

Nina Well, I can smell you from here but I'm not bragging about it.

Tommy Curt ... what d'you wanna do, mate?

Curtis I ... I don't know.

Sarah Jez has a proposition for you. Don't you, Jez?

Jez I do?

Sarah Yes. Jez wants to say he won't write about anything that happens here. He won't take any more photos. Everything that happens here remains ... oh, what's the phrase?

Jez Off the record?

Sarah Off the record. That goes for all of us. Right?

Nina Of course.

Sarah Alex?

Alex I'm here to support you. That's all.

Sarah Jez?

Jez ... Okay. But on one condition.

Tommy No conditions.

Curtis It's all right, Tom! (*At* **Jez**.) Go on.

Jez You give me an interview. Exclusive. 'How I Changed from Nice Boy to Nazi Boy.'

Curtis I'm not a Nazi.

Alex Your nose is growing.

Curtis I'm bloody not!

Tommy None of us are!

Gavin That's right.

Sarah Okay, okay. He won't use the word Nazi.

Tommy Not fascist either.

Sarah No words like that. Right, Jez?

Jez You can describe your political beliefs in whatever way you like. I won't be judgemental.

Gavin Oh, yeah, and he can trust you.

Jez Well, yes, he bloody can actually.

Tommy You know how I've been described? By the local gazette? 'A henchman.' My mum was livid.

Jez I will not misquote or misrepresent anything Curtis says.

Slight pause.

Alex Ashamed of your views, Curtis?

Curtis I'm not ashamed of anything.

Gavin Wayne won't approve this. No way.

Jez You gonna be bossed around by this Munchkin?

Gavin Who're you calling a . . . whatever it was?

Slight pause.

Curtis *starts to hold out his hand to* **Jez**.

Gavin Wait! What if they put you on the cover?

Curtis Eh?

Gavin It's a magazine for sexual perverts.You want everyone to think you . . . bat for the other side?

Alex 'Bat for the other side'?

Jez It has a quaint charm.

Curtis You'll make it clear that I'm . . . you know.

Jez Fascist but straight. You've got it.

Gavin Normal! Say he's normal!

Tommy Nationalist and heterosexual will do.

Jez Okay, okay, whatever.

Curtis Deal!

Curtis *and* **Jez** *shake hands.*

Alex You've no idea where that hand was last night.

Curtis *pulls hand away.*

Jez, **Sarah** *and* **Link** *laugh.*

Gavin It's disgusting – Why's that funny, eh? Where's the bloody joke?

Alex Perhaps *you're* the bloody joke.

Gavin Yeah? You think?

Tommy Okay! Chairs! How many we need?

Nina Everyone in the room needs to take part. No spectators allowed. I, as you see, have come fully equipped. One of the bonuses of breaking your back when you're ten. You save a fortune on furniture for the rest of your life.

Tommy So that's . . . eight.

Curtis Not him.

Points at **Link**.

Alex Why?

Curtis He's sod all to do with any of this.

Gavin (*at* **Link**) You! Out!

Link This is *my* place!

Alex He goes, I go.

Jez She goes, I go.

Sarah Need we carry on?

Curtis Bloody hell, sell tickets, why don't you!

Tommy Okay. Eight chairs.

Curtis Seven.

Tommy But I thought you said –

Curtis Gavin's waiting downstairs.

Gavin Eh? I'm *what*?

Curtis I want you to keep watch.

Gavin For what?

Tommy Just follow instructions, mate.

Gavin Nah, nah, hang on! Immigrants, cripples and perverts can be part of it but *I've* got to wait outside like a . . . a . . .

Alex Messy pup?

Gavin Shut up!

Tommy All Curtis means is –

Gavin He can explain himself, I think.

Curtis I'm just . . . I'm just nervous Wayne might find out and come here and –

Gavin How? He thinks we're canvassing the Tube stations. 'Our mobiles'll be out of contact for a couple of hours, Wayne.' That's what I told him. What you told me to tell him. Why me? Cos he trusts me. Wayne believes everything I decide to tell him.

Curtis . . . Look, Gav –

Gavin Sod the lot of you!

Heads for front door.

Curtis Tom?!

Tommy Wait, Gav!

Slight pause.

Gavin . . . Well?

Curtis Mate. I'm sorry. Come here.

Gavin Why don't *you* come *here*?

Slight pause.

Curtis *goes to* **Gavin**.

Curtis I wasn't thinking. I've been at my wits' end lately. You know that, don't you? None of this would've been possible without you. Would it, Tom, eh?

Tommy No way.

Gavin I got a lot of votes pledged this afternoon. I bet Wayne'd be pleased if he knew how good I was getting on.

Curtis I'll tell him.

Gavin Perhaps a promotion.

Curtis Perhaps, yeah.

Gavin Perhaps *definitely*.

Curtis . . . Yes.

Gavin Chairs!

Curtis Tommy!

Tommy Pronto!

Tommy *and* **Gavin** *rush out.*

Nina Mmm . . . Ocean Spray!

Alex With a hint of pig.

Nina He can wrap his salty rashers round me any day.

Sarah Nina!

Nina I know. I despise myself – Curtis! Down to business! Tell me about him!

Curtis Tom's my best mate.

Nina Not Mr Ocean Spray! Your dead brother. Jason. That's why we're all here.

Link So it's your *real* brother! Jason! *He's* the ghost!

Nina I prefer the word 'spirit', my dear – Sarah, where's my inspirational crystal?

Sarah *gets crystal from bag and gives it to* **Nina**.

Link Are you gonna ... contact Jason's spirit?

Nina If I can, yes.

Sarah Nina made contact with a girl in the library.

Nina She'd died in a fire there about fifty years ago.

Sarah She wanted to know the end to a book she'd been reading.

Jez Did you tell her?

Nina Out of print unfortunately.

Link (*at* **Curtis**) Was your real brother murdered like your real dad?

Slight pause.

Curtis I ... I don't think I can do this.

Nina Don't be silly. People's bodies stop working all the time. Don't get all wishy-washy about it.

Curtis But I can't –

Nina Listen, sweetie! I've just made my way up an Everest of Dog Turds to get here. I did that because I thought you wanted a seance.

Sarah He does! – Curt? When I told you about Nina you said you wanted to try this.

Curtis I did. I *do*.

Nina Curtis ... I know it's hard. You have to open up and talk about things. Things you haven't talked about in years. Perhaps never. It's scary. Right?

Curtis ... Yeah.

Link You know what my mate says? We only regret the things we don't do.

Pause.

Curtis ... Okay. No regrets. Let's do it.

Nina Jason! He died six years ago. That right?

Curtis ... Yeah. Six years ago.

Slight pause.

Nina And? Come on! More!

Link He did pictures.

Nina Eh? What's that?

Curtis Jason – he painted pictures.

Link They're in the back room.

Sarah My God! They're still there!

Rushes for bedroom, then reconsiders, hesitates.

Curtis I know. Me too.

Sarah You couldn't ... ?

Curtis No.

Sarah Strange.

Curtis Yeah.

Sarah Too ...

Curtis Real.

Sarah Yeah.

Jez (*at* **Alex**) You understanding any of this?

Alex Yeah. Flirt alert.

Sarah Shut up, Al!

Nina Dead brother!

Sarah Jason told him stories.

Jez From books?

Curtis No. Jason ... he sort of made them up ...

Nina Go on. I'm beginning to feel his karma.

Caresses crystal.

Curtis When I was a kid – I mean, really young – I used to have trouble getting to sleep. Things used to scare me. Sound of next door's telly. Jason used to tell me stories to calm me down.

Jez About what?

Curtis Kings and queens.

Sarah Witches and dragons.

Link Fairy stories.

A distant door gets kicked in.

Dogs bark.

Sarah He used to mix fantasy up with real stuff. Didn't he, Curt?

Nina How'd you mean?

Curtis The stories. He used to put real places and people in them.

Sarah Your mum – she became the Queen.

Curtis Jason – he was the Prince. Or sometimes it was me.

Jez Prince Curtis!

Nina Sarah says you couldn't find any photos of him.

Curtis We lost a lot of stuff when we moved out of here.

Alex You lost *every* photo of your brother?

Curtis Not *just* him! All our photos were in one box. We lost the box.

Sarah You can't blame Curt. He was only twelve at the time.

Nina It would have been so useful to have some . . . visual image.

Sarah That's why I've brought this.

Searches in bag

Curtis Sarah?

Sarah The day we went to the fair. Remember?

Takes photo from bag.

Curtis I didn't know you had that.

Sarah I only found it recently.

Alex You told me you chucked out everything to do with him.

Sarah Did I?

Alex Yes!

Sarah Then I lied, didn't I!

Holds photo out to **Curtis**.

Pause.

Curtis *takes photo.*

Curtis ... Sarah ... It's Jason.

Sarah ... You okay?

Curtis ... Yeah.

Jez Let me see.

Nina Me! Me!

Curtis *hands photo to* **Nina**.

Nina Oh, Sarah! Look at you!

Jez *and* **Alex** *gather round to look.*

Sarah I was bit chubby then.

Jez You were gorgeous

Alex She *is* gorgeous! A liar, but gorgeous.

Nina (*at* **Curtis**) You were a midget.

Sarah He shot up all at once.

Jez 'Shot up all at once.' Oh, lordy!

Alex Give it a rest.

Sarah It's funny ... when I think of Jason, he's always so old. Like really grown up. Like my dad or something. But look at him. He's young. Not much older than we are now.

Nina When was this taken?

Sarah The year he died.

Nina So Jason's ... how old?

Sarah Nineteen. Curtis is twelve. I'm eleven.

Nina And ... cut Jason's hair? Who is it?

Jez They could be twins.

Looks at **Curtis**.

Nina And where did you say it was taken?

Sarah Victoria Park. They used to have a fair there every spring.

Alex Still do.

Sarah But they were so much ... *more*, then. Brighter. Louder.

Nina You're just getting old, my dear. That's all.

Sarah Jason – he made friends with someone who worked there. Didn't he, Curt?

Curtis ... Yeah, that's right.

Sarah He had a strange name ...

Curtis A nickname.

Sarah Yeah ... What was it?

Curtis Something to do with ... spinnning.

Sarah Yes! Spinning ... round and round ...

Curtis Spiral!

Sarah Spiral! That's it! He worked on the –

Curtis *and* **Sarah** – the merry-go-round!

Sarah That's why we got all those rides for free. Yes! Yes!

Curtis Dolphins!

Sarah What?

Curtis The merry-go-round. We sat on these big –

Sarah *and* **Curtis** – dolphins!

Curtis Blue dolphins!

Sarah And the moon, Curt. Remember? It had that big moon above.

Curtis A mirrorball.

Sarah Was it?

Curtis Yeah. It sparkled everywhere.

Sarah We tried to catch the sparkles – Moonbeams!

Curtis Moonbeams! That's what we called them!

Sarah If we catch enough we can turn them into jewels.

Curtis I've caught one!

Sarah Me too!

Curtis *and* **Sarah** *gaze at each other, lost in the bubble of their remembrance.*

Pause.

The bubble bursts as –

Tommy *and* **Gavin** *come in holding two chairs each.*

Tommy Okay. We struck lucky on the floor below.

Sarah Well done, Tommy.

Tommy I've wiped 'em down with a bit of old curtain, but double-check before you sit. We'll search another floor.

Sarah I don't mind standing.

Alex Nor do I.

Nina You have to sit. That's the rules. No spectators and everyone sitting in a circle and holding hands. The spirits get very stroppy if things ain't done properly. And it's me they'll take it out on. Believe me, I don't fancy an ancient Aboriginal blowing his didgeridoo in my ear at three in the morning.

Looks at **Tommy**.

Nina You can blow your didgeridoo in my ear any time, Ocean Spray.

Tommy Gav!

Heads for door.

Gavin I'm bloody knackered!

Tommy You need to get fit!

Tommy *and* **Gavin** *leave.*

Nina He wiped the chairs – Oh, what a considerate love!

Sarah Neen!

Nina Your brother's death!

Pause.

Come on, come on.

Curtis Gimme a second! I need to get it . . . into some kind of order. You don't live life as a story, do you? You live it as life. The stories happen later.

Jez Oh, that's good.

Takes notebook from bag and scribbles in it.

Sarah Off the record! Remember?

Holds out hand.

Jez But it's a gem!

Sarah You gave your word!

Jez *gives her notebook.*

Sarah Curtis?

Curtis Jason had been looking after me since our dad died.

Nina Which was . . . ?

Jez It happened when Curtis was eleven. Must have been the year before that photo. Sorry.

Curtis My mum . . . she went off the rails a bit.

Sarah It was clinical depression, Curt.

Link My mate gets that. He says it's like falling into a dark pit.

Sarah It is.

Link Once I touched his hand and he cried.

Curtis Mum started bringing stray dogs into the flat. She wasn't eating properly . . . Wasn't washing . . . Me and Jason – we were so scared for her.

Sarah But your mum got better as soon as she met Mr Avalon.

Curtis Oh, yeah.

Nina How long after your dad dying did she meet Mr Avalon?

Curtis Nine months.

Jez Where did they meet?

Curtis In the doctor's surgery. They were both waiting to see the same doctor. They started talking and – Wham! Love at first sight, I guess. Mum – she changed over night.

Sarah She was her old self again.

Curtis *Better* than her old self. It was brilliant. Jason was over the moon. He could get on with his life now. He'd put so much on hold to look after me. He didn't apply for art school. And he could've done. Mr Avalon knew that Jason wanted to travel so he gave him some money to go anywhere in the world. Explore. It was a dream come true for Jason. He couldn't stop talking about it. Remember, Sarah?

Sarah Do I?! All those maps. The big compass.

Jez Where did he go?

Curtis The Colombian Jungle.

Link I'd love to go there!

Curtis Jason wanted to see the Lost City. God, he was so excited. He was gonna hike it. More of an adventure, he said. He talked me through the route night after night. The Sierra Nevada Mountains. We took him to the airport. Me, Mum, Mr Avalon and Wayne. Jason was crying buckets. He kept saying, 'I've got to do this, Curt. I'll miss you. But I've gotta go.' I was crying too. I'd never cried like that before. Not even when Dad died. I hung on to Jason's jacket. I didn't wanna let go. Mr Avalon said, 'Don't worry. You'll see him again.' They had to pull me away from him. I was screaming. Mr Avalon told Jason to run. Jason went through the checkout . . . he turned round to look at me . . . He was crying . . . then he . . . he disappeared . . .

Visibly distressed, he goes to balcony.

A distant door is kicked in.

Dogs bark.

Jez *sneakily aims camera at* **Curtis**.

Sarah (*under her breath*) Jez!

Jez *looks at* **Sarah**.

Sarah *holds hand out for camera.*

Slight pause.

Jez *gives camera to* **Sarah**.

Jez Spoilsport.

Sarah Hypocrite.

Nina (*at* **Sarah**) Get lover boy back. I need to know more.

Sarah *I* can tell you. And he's *not* lover boy.

Alex No?

Sarah No!

Slight pause.

Nina Okay. So Jason has disappeared through the checkout and flown off to . . . where was it again?

Link Colombian Jungle.

Jez Lost City.

Sarah There were a few postcards from him. Fantastic pictures on them. Flowers big as . . . that armchair. Monkeys. Sunsets you wouldn't believe. The last postcard said not to worry if it goes quiet for a while as he's about to enter the jungle and, as far as he knew, there weren't many post offices along the way. We all laughed at that.

Link And *did* it go quiet?

Sarah Yeah. A few weeks went by. A month. Two months. Not a word from him. No one worried. All Curtis talked about was Jason coming back. 'I hope he's back for the wedding. He's gotta be here for the wedding.'

Nina That's the wedding of Mr Avalon and Curtis's mum?

Sarah Yeah, she'd moved in with him.

Nina In sin! What fun!

Sarah They'd started moving everyone out of this place by then so . . . well, I suppose it was the obvious thing to do.

And Mr Avalon's politics weren't so ... focused as they are now. I remember he talked about the Blitz spirit and land of hope and glory and all that. We all thought he was a bit of a joke. But I do remember one time ... I forget when exactly. But it was early on. I was sitting in the living room with Curtis. Mr Avalon was spouting off about how his wife – his first wife – had had to wait ages for hospital treatment. 'It's the immigrants sapping the National Health,' he kept saying. 'They killed my wife.'

Nina What did she die of?

Sarah Some cancer thing.

Jez Leukaemia.

Sarah That's it. Wayne once told me his dad hardly ever visited his first wife. Mr Avalon hated hospitals. It was all left up to Wayne. Must've been terrible for him. She died in the same month as Curtis's dad. It's what bonded Mr Avalon and Curtis's mum so quick. They kept talking about fate and stuff. You know? Both mourning the death of a spouse.

Jez Both blossoming fascists.

Sarah No! Not Curtis's mum.

Jez But she is!

Sarah You didn't see her after the murder.

Alex What's that got to do with it?

Sarah She was a wreck, Alex. Neighbours pointing at her. Kids calling her names. I don't blame her for clinging onto anything that could save her. I'm not saying I agree with it. But if you ask me if I'd prefer to see her like she is now or how she was after the murder I'd take now any day. I grew up with her. I lived three floors below. This was like a second home to me.

Alex Perhaps you see it different after you've dated a fascist.

Sarah I did *not* date a fascist!

Alex You forgotten that speech?

Sarah And that's when it ended! But until then ... oh, it all crept up so slowly.

Alex I saw it coming a mile off.

Sarah You saw a boy! That's all! Politics had nothing to do with it!

Alex What's that supposed to mean?

Sarah You know!

Alex No! *You* tell *me*!

Nina Let's get back to the task in hand, shall we?

Slight pause.

Sarah, my dear?

Sarah ... There was a telegram. It said Jason had gone missing.

Nina In the jungle?

Sarah Yes.

Nina And then?

Sarah It's hard to ... remember the order of things.

Jez They found a skull or something, didn't they?

Sarah That's right. Thanks, Jez. Mr Avalon got a letter. It said a skull had been found by the edge of a river.

Link Just a skull?

Nina Did they carry out tests?

Sarah Yeah. Mr Avalon showed Curtis every bit of information he got. The tests were one hundred per cent certain.

Jez Jason was toast.

Link But to find just a skull? What could've happened to him?

Sarah No one was sure. It was assumed he was walking along this ledge by a river and he ... he must have slipped and fallen in and ... hit by a speedboat propeller ...

Jez Eaten by crocodiles.

Sarah Don't, Jez!

Nina It's a possibility, my dear.

Sarah I just hope it was quick, that's all. Whatever happened. I hope he didn't suffer.

Tommy *comes in with two chairs.*

Tommy Okay. Nearly there. Gav's searching the lower floors for some more.

Nina Look at those arms. Let me feel your muscles, Ocean Spray ... Come on! I don't bite.

Feels **Tommy***'s arms.*

Nina Let's skip the small talk. How'd you fancy a date with a mermaid? If you kiss me – who knows? I might start to walk and dance the rumba.

Slight pause.

Tommy ... Where's Curtis?

Sarah *indicates balcony.*

Tommy Should I ... ?

Sarah *shakes her head.*

Sarah Perhaps you can tell Nina about the ghost, Tom. The first time Curtis saw it.

Nina Were you with him, darling?

Tommy Yeah. I'd been at the –

Sarah Hang on – Jez?

Holds out hands for tape recorder.

Jez But I'm not –

Sarah I don't trust you.

Jez *gives tape recorder to* **Sarah**.

Sarah Go on, Tom.

Tommy I'd been boxing at the York Hall. Curtis came. Never misses.

Nina I bet you look gorgeous in your shorts.

Jez In the showers!

Nina Be still my heart!

Sarah You win the fight, Tom?

Tommy A knockout!

Sarah *and* **Nina** Yesss!

Tommy We went for an Indian afterwards.

Alex The joys of multiculturism, eh?

Sarah Not now, Alex! – Tom?

Tommy . . . We got back to Curtis's place about midnight. We went up to his room. We were playing some music. Curtis got up to pull the curtains and – I heard him gasp! I looked up at him. I thought he was going to faint. I said, 'What's up, mate?' He said, 'Tom! Look!' He pointed to the other side of the road. 'It's Jason! Jason's ghost!' I looked out the window.

Nina What did you see?

Tommy The other side of the road.

Jez What about Jason?

Tommy That's what I mean. All I saw was the other side of the road. No ghost.

Nina But Curtis had seen it.

Tommy Oh, yeah. You should've seen him. He kept saying, 'I've just seen Jason! I've just seen Jason.' He wanted me to stay the night. I said, 'Sure.' I've got my own Z bed in his room. I kept awake and made sure he was safe.

Sarah Oh, Tom.

Nina How far away is the other side of the road?

Jez Twenty yards.

Nina And is it well lit?

Tommy Not really.

Nina So why's Curtis so sure he saw Jason's ghost?

Gavin *enters – breathless and sweating – with two chairs.*

Tommy Well done, Gav.

Gavin Yeah, yeah.

Nina Can you smell – oh, Dopey's walked something in.

Gavin Eh? What?

Tommy Check your shoes, mate.

Gavin *checks his shoes.*

Jez Ugh.

Alex You smell like your politics.

Gavin Shut up!

Nina Sarah, where's my eau de toilette?

Sarah Here, Neen.

Get it from **Nina**'s *bag.*

Nina *sprays herself.*

The others are all laughing at **Gavin**.

Alex Messy pup!

Jez You should stay outside.

Gavin Shut up! Shut up!

Link It's supposed to be lucky.

Gavin *punches* **Link** *hard.*

Link *stumbles back and falls.*

General cries etc from everyone.

Jez *rushes at* **Gavin**.

Jez You bloody bastard.

Gets **Gavin** *in armlock.*

Gavin I'll fucking kill you.

Jez Come on, then! Come on.

Gavin *can't free himself.*

Jez I'll snap your fucking arm off!

Curtis *has rushed in.*

Curtis What's going on!

Sarah Gavin hit Link.

Gavin He was laughing at me – Ahhh!

Jez *has twisted* **Gavin***'s arm.*

Link *is on his feet. His nose is bleeding.*

Sarah We were *all* laughing at you! Wanna hit me too? Come on!

Nina What about me? I'm more your size!

Curtis (*at* **Jez**) Let him go.

Slight pause.

Jez *lets go of* **Gavin**.

Link I'm gonna get my mate. You'll be sorry.

Gavin Get him! He don't scare me!

Link *runs out of flat.*

Alex Link!

Sarah Link!

Jez Come back, mate.

Gavin Bloody vagrant. Should've cleared off in the first place.

Jez *steps towards* **Gavin**.

Gavin *steps back.*

Jez Pig!

Curtis Get out!

Gavin (*at* **Jez**) You heard!

Curtis Not him! *You!*

Gavin Wh- what?

Tommy Curt?

Curtis I know what I'm doing! – You've been warned, Gav. Out!

Gavin Warned? Me?

Steps towards **Curtis**.

Tommy *stands in front of* **Gavin**.

Tommy Careful, Gavin.

Gavin Oh yeah. Your true colours are out now, ain't they? I've warned Wayne about you. Both of you. You don't see me in the gym, do you? Oh no. I'm just there to collect your spit in a bucket. You look right through me. But I'm there. I hear you talk. You ain't one of us. Neither of you. It ain't in your blood.

Curtis Get. Out!

Slight pause.

Gavin *leaves.*

Pause.

Curtis Come on. Let's get on with it. Quick!

Nina You're sure it was Jason's ghost you saw?

Curtis No doubt.

Nina Why?

Curtis The jacket.

Nina What jacket?

Sarah The sparkle jacket.

Curtis That's what we called it.

Sarah We were only kids.

Curtis Jason was given a jacket.

Sarah A present.

Curtis Spiral!

Sarah What?

Curtis I remember now. It was a present from Spiral!

Sarah You're right! Oh, God.

Nina There's lots of jackets, my darlings.

Sarah Oh, not like this, Neen.

Curtis It'd had those silver stud things on it.

Sarah All over.

Curtis Swirling shapes.

Sarah Some of them were coloured.

Curtis Like jewels.

Sarah It was beautiful.

Curtis Weighed a ton.

Sarah There was painting on it too.

Curtis Round the collar.

Sarah On the back.

Curtis Sleeves

Nina What of?

Curtis Dophins.

Sarah Moons.

Curtis All done by hand.

Sarah Unique, Nina, unique.

Curtis Jason was wearing it at the airport. When I said goodbye. The jacket I was clutching on to – Nina, it's my brother's ghost I saw. I know it was. And I've seen him three times since then. Twice more outside the house. And once outside the community hall after Wayne's speech. The ghost was standing in the estate opposite. It was in the shadowes. I saw the jacket sparkle. I pushed through the crows to chase after it. Some people were knocked to the floor. Local press took photos. Wayne and Stacey did their nut.

Nina Did you tell them about the ghost?

Curtis Wayne and Stacey? Jesus, no. Tommy's the only one.

Nina The turd-foot dwarf seems to know.

Tommy That was an accident.

Curtis He heard me and Tommy talking.

Tommy We had to involve him.

Curtis I hated him knowing. Didn't I, Tom?

Tommy You did, mate.

Curtis But ... there was no choice. I had to go ahead with ... what we're doing now. If I didn't ... It's been doing my head in.

Tommy His hands wouldn't stop shaking.

Sarah They still are.

Tommy That's why I phoned you.

Alex Yeah. Why *her* exactly?

Tommy Cos my mate needed help.

Alex Well, *she's* my mate and I don't appreciate *you* digging up –

Tommy I don't give a toss! I'd do anything for him.

Alex Well, I'd do anything for her and she don't need you coming along and –

Sarah Stop it! Stop it! I *wanted* to come, Alex! I told you. I didn't want to turn a corner one day and ... see him when I wasn't ready! Okay? Now, put a sock in it!

Nina Cover the windows! Chairs round the table! It's time to talk to the dead!

They start to find ways of covering the windows.

Most of the boards can be put back in place.

A blanket is used for the balcony window.

Much noisy activity and bustle as –

Hang it over the curtain rail! ... That's it! Just lean that board against the – Yes! Good! There's still light there! ... That'll have to do ... The chairs! Come on!

The chairs have been put in place.

They are gathering round the table.

Sit!

Curtis *sits in between* **Nina** *and* **Sarah**.

Alex *swaps places with* **Jez** *so she can be on the other side of* **Sarah**.

This means **Tommy** *is now sitting next to* **Jez**.

Nina Hands!

Tommy *hesitates at holding* **Jez**'s *hand.*

The others watch.

Slight pause.

Tommy *holds* **Jez**'s *hand.*

Nina Spirits! Hear our cry! We are in search of Jason. Brother to Curtis. He passed into your world six years ago. Please help us, oh, spirits. Something is troubling Jason. I have sensed secrets. Please, spirits. Guide Jason to us.

Nothing happens.

Pause.

Spirits! Please … Guide Jason to us!

Nothing happens.

Pause.

Jez My belly's rumbling.

Sarah Shhh!

The table jolts!

Everyone gasps, leans back, etc.

Nina Don't lose the circle!

They touch hands again.

Jason!

The table jolts.

Jez Oh God …

Tommy Curt?

Curtis I'm all right – Sarah?

Sarah I'm okay.

Nina I … feel something. Yes … oh, yes. Something is getting closer … closer … Jason! … Jason … Jason …

Zak *has appeared in the doorway. He is twenty-two years old and wearing jeans, boots, T-shirt and a jacket decorated with silver studs and paint (exactly as described by* **Curtis** *and* **Sarah***).*

Sarah *sees* **Zak** *and –*

She gets to her feet.

Alex Babe?

Everyone now sees **Zak**.

They gasp, cry out, some stand, etc.

Then they freeze.

Slight pause.

Nina Blimey! It worked!

Sarah . . . N-Nina?

Nina There's nothing to be afraid of!

Jez You've gotta be kidding.

Nina *wheels towards the figure.*

Nina Oh, spirit of Jason! Why are you so troubled?

They stare at **Zak**.

Zak *is staring at* **Curtis**.

Link *runs in, breathless.*

Link Zak! Zak!

Looks round room.

It's . . . okay. It's . . . it's not any . . . of these.

Goes to **Tommy**.

Where's your mate gone?

Tommy *cannot answer.*

Link Where is he? Zak wants to teach him a lesson.

Nina There . . . there was an argument, my dear.

Sarah Gavin's not here, Link.

Link Lucky for him. My mate was gonna – what was it you said, Zak? Grind his bones to make your bread!

Notices the way everyone is staring at **Zak**.

Link What's going on?

Sarah . . . Curt?

Slight pause.

Then –

Curtis *hurriedly knocks boards from windows etc.*

Setting sunlight fills the room.

Slight pause.

Zak *is gazing at* **Curtis** *as if in a trance.*

Jez It's not Jason, is it?

Sarah No, no.

Link It's Zak.

Sarah But that jacket – It's Jason's!

Alex It can't be.

Sarah It is! It is! – Curt?

Curtis (*at* **Zak**) . . . Where did you get that jacket?

Link He's had it ages. Since before I met him – Ain't you?

Slight pause.

Zak? Why ain't you saying anything?

Slight pause.

Slowly, **Curtis** *approaches* **Zak**.

Zak *reaches out to touch* **Curtis***'s cheek.*

Curtis *slaps his hand away.*

The slap brings **Zak** *out of his 'trance'.*

Zak *looks around at others.*

Slight pause.

Zak *clicks into action and starts packing bags.*

Link Zak? . . . What's going on?

Zak *indicates* **Link** *should start packing.*

Link We going? Why? I thought we liked it here.

Zak *indicates* **Link** *should start packing.*

Slight pause.

Link *starts packing.*

Others watch.

Slight pause.

Nina Jason gave you that jacket, didn't he?

Zak *freezes.*

Jez Oh, lordy.

Sarah Is it true, Zak?

Nina Oh, it's true. Right, Zak?

Link Zak?

Zak *resumes packing.*

Slight pause.

Sarah Did you . . . did you meet him in the jungle?

Link Zak ain't been to no jungle.

Nina Is that true?

Link He's never been abroad – Have you?

Zak *continues packing.*

Nina Do you know how Jason died?

Zak *freezes.*

Jez Oh, lordy.

Alex He knows.

Sarah Oh, Curt.

Zak *picks up bag and heads for front door.*

Link Hang on! We ain't packed everything yet! The books!

Zak *puts his arm round* **Link**.

Zak *and* **Link** *head for door –*

Sarah No! You can't go!

Nina Please stay!

Sarah Curt! *Curt!*

Curtis Don't go!

Zak *freezes.*

Curtis You can't go and . . . not tell me! Don't think you'll upset me. You won't. I've imagined so many things about how Jason died. Each one worse than the last. No matter how bad it was I'd rather . . . I'd rather just know. Zak. I need to know what happened to my brother . . . Please.

Zak *turns to face* **Curtis**.

Zak I . . . I can't tell you.

Curtis Why?

Zak I made a promise.

Cutis To who?

Slight pause.

Nina To Jason?

Zak . . . Yes.

Turns to leave again –

Nina Jason didn't die in the jungle, did he?

Zak *freezes.*

Jez Oh, lordy.

Curtis Of *course* he died in the bloody jungle. What you going on about?

Nina Your brother went to the jungle with that jacket, you said. Now it's here on this bloke and he's never been abroad. *You* work it out.

Curtis Jason went to the airport. I waved goodbye to him.

Sarah But the jacket's here, Curt! Look!

Curtis The authorities sent photos of where my brother went missing. Sarah, you saw them. My dad showed us.

Sarah Not your dad! *Avalon*!

Curtis They sent cremated remains, for chrissakes. We threw them from the roof of this place. Jason's dead! Six years ago. In the Colombian Jungle . . . Perhaps that ain't his jacket.

Sarah You *know* it is.

Jez Did Jason . . . did he fake his own death?

Zak No!

Sarah Then *what*, Zak? *What?*

Nina You've got to tell us, my dear.

Jez We'll keep on guessing and guessing till you do.

Nina You *want* to tell us, don't you!

Zak Yes! Of course I bloody want to! It's eating me up.

Link You're upsetting him. Leave him alone.

Holds **Zak**.

Nina Why did you come here, Zak?

Zak Because … because I wanted to feel close to … someone again. To see the things they grew up with … To see the people they spoke about and … I can't explain it. You have to … love someone … and lose them. Lose someone so special it's like … gravity going. Nothing to hold you on the planet any more. You won't understand that.

Sarah Oh, I do.

Curtis Me too.

Nina *wheels closer to* **Zak**.

Nina Listen, my dear. The thing that's eating you up. It's like piranhas in your belly. And piranhas are ravenous things. Their little jaws keep nibbling and nibbling and nibbling. In the end, they'll eat so much of you there'll be nothing left. What's the cure? To spit the piranhas out. Here! Now!

Zak But I can't, I can't. I promised Jason. I promised … I'd never tell.

Sarah Why don't you do what Jason used to do? Tell us a story.

Link Yeah! A fairy story!

Nina Oh, very good.

Jez Of course! After all, a fairy story ain't real life, is it?

Alex Not real life at all.

Nina And if we … well, if we deduce things from that story …

Sarah Well, that ain't Zak's fault, is it?

Nina He wouldn't've broke any promise.

Sarah None at all.

Jez None.

Alex No way.

Curtis Please, Zak ... I need to hear the story.

Slight pause.

Link Show them what you can do, Zak. What *we* can do! Street entertainers supreme! Come on! Showtime!

Has climbed up on table.

Ladies and gentlemen! Roll up, roll up! Spare us a few minutes of your time and enter a world of enchantment and wonder.

Nina Very good!

Wheels closer to table.

Link We bring you stories! Fantasy. Thriller. Thriller-fantasy. Comedy-weepie-fantasy! Zak here will spin a tale of surprise and magic before your very eyes. Nothing is prepared. Just call out three things and Zak will spin a web of a story to take your breath away. Come on! Don't be shy. This is an experience not to be missed. Three things. Anything you like ... Who'll gimme the first?

Others are gathering round.

Nina A prince called Jason!

Slight pause.

Link ... Okay. First thing! A prince called Jason! Next?

Sarah A jacket that sparkles.

Link Second thing! A jacket that sparkles! Oh, this is gonna be a challenge, O Storyteller. One more!

Curtis ... A death!

Link ... Okay! Zak, O! Great Storyteller! Your storytelling challenge has been set. A story with a prince called Jason. A jacket that sparkles. And death. Tell us this story, O plot-weaving wizard.

Jumps off table.

Slight pause.

Slowly, **Zak** *gets up onto table.*

Others are sitting round table like an audience.

The setting sunlight is now very intense.

For a while **Zak** *does nothing.*

Then, abruptly, it's showtime –

Zak There was once a king and queen.

Link We're off!

Zak The King and Queen had a son. Prince Jason!

Link The first thing! Well done, O Storyteller!

Zak One day Prince Jason looked out of the window and saw everything had turned white. Snow. He'd never seen it before. He rushed outside to play.

Link Where did he go, Storyteller?

Zak Prince Jason went to the forest, my inquisitive Apprentice. He climbed trees and knocked icicles from branches. He made snowmen. He made snow angels. He played all day. When he got home his lips had turned bright blue and he lay on his bed as motionless as a statue. A layer of frost covered his skin. The King and Queen started a big log fire in his room but, no matter how hot the room got, the layer of frost remained on Prince Jason.

Link Something is wrong with the Prince! Oh, what a twist! We're captivated already! What happens next! Tell us, O Storyteller!

Zak A witch!

Link Of course! Why?

Zak The King went to a witch and asked her to cure whatever was ailing the Prince. The Witch said, 'Prince

Jason has snow in the bones. There is only one cure I know of. You must go to the Wild Orchard at the edge of the Kingdom and pick him some lemons from the tallest tree.'

Link Lemons? To make . . . a lemon drink?

The others are beginning to visibly react now.

They recognise the death of **Curtis***'s dad in the story.*

They glance at **Curtis**.

Zak But there was something the Witch forgot to warn the King about – Come on, Apprentice!

Link What did the Witch forget to warn the King about?

Zak The Dragon, my ever-attentive Apprentice. The Dragon that protected the Wild Orchard. And when this Dragon saw the King picking lemons it swooped down on the King. The King cried out. The Dragon raised its claws – seven of them – and . . . it stabbed the King.

Link Did the King die, Storyteller?

Zak Eventually. But first he walked all the way back to the castle.

Link Leaving a trail of blood in the snow.

Zak Then the King climbed the steps in tower.

Link A rose petal of blood on every step.

Zak The King got to the top of the tower. The King went to Prince Jason's room. The King gave the magic lemons to his sick son. And then –

Link The King fell down dead.

Zak In front of his son!

Link And was Prince Jason cured?

Zak Yes. But – oh, the guilt Prince Jason felt, my Apprentice. The King is dead all because Prince Jason got snow in the bones. And now – oh, more guilt for the Prince.

Link What, O Storyteller?!

Zak The King's death sent the Queen mad. She started to bring wolves into the castle. She cried, 'My precious wolves. They are all I need.'

Everyone is beginning to react more and more:

Lots of glances, tiny gasps, nods.

Lots of looks towards **Curtis**.

Curtis *is looking increasingly agitated.*

Zak Prince Jason couldn't bear to see the Queen so distressed. He went on long walks. He walked to parts of the Kingdom he'd never been to before. One day he found himself by the edge of a – oh my!

Link What?

Zak It's a lagoon. The water is smooth as glass and blue as cornflowers.

Link I see it!

Zak The Prince sits beside it. A young man comes up and sits beside the Prince and says, 'You know, there's a legend about this lagoon. It says that dolphins will appear whenever two people who are in love with each other are reflected in the water.'

Link What's this young man called, O Storyteller?!

Zak He's called . . . Spiral. Prince Jason and Spiral sit by the edge of the lagoon and talk. They talk all day and into the night. They talk like they have never talked to anyone before. Like they've known each other all their lives. Then they hold each other. Then they kiss each other. They look at their reflections on the surface of the lagoon. And . . . dolphins appear.

Slight pause.

Back to the Queen!

Link Wolves!

Zak No!

Link No?

Zak The Queen has met a New King now. The Queen is in love with this New King. They plan to get married.

Link Stop press! Queen to marry New King!

Zak But there's a problem.

Link Tell us!

Zak The lagoon. Moonlight. Stars. Prince Jason says to Spiral. 'I've never felt like this towards . . . another boy. You've made me feel lots of new things. Up until now my life has been in neat boxes. All of them ordered and labelled. But you . . . you have come along and blown all the boxes apart. I want us to get as close as possible in all possible ways.' And Spiral says, 'I feel the same. That's why I have made you a gift to celebrate what we have created together . . .'

Link What is it, O Storyteller?!

Zak 'Once a month the dolphins collect moonlight from the surface of the lagoon. This moonlight is the most precious thing in the whole world. I have woven it into this garment, my Prince. See how it sparkles. Please put on . . . It is called Moonfleece!'

Link The second thing! A jacket that sparkles! Well done, Storyteller!

Zak Many thanks, sweet Apprentice – But aren't you missing something?

Link What?

Zak I mentioned a problem.

Link Forgive me, O Storyteller! What is this problem you mentioned?

Zak The New King says to the Queen, 'There must be a reason why our lives went so wrong.' The Queen says, 'I agree, but what could it have been?' The New King says, 'Well, my wife died when the moon was full.' The Queen says, 'I think the moon was full when my husband was killed too.' The New King says, 'That's it! Don't you see? The moon is to blame for everything.' The Queen says, 'Goodness! I've been so blind.' The New King says, 'We'll create a new kingdom without anything to do with the moon! People who like the moon will be banished. All references to the moon will be taken out of the books. If the moon shines at night people must close their windows. If they happen to catch sight of it they must abuse it. And we will name this new kingdom after me. We will call it Avalon!' – You see the problem, sweet Apprentice?

Slight pause.

Apprentice?!

Link Yes. I see the problem. Prince Jason is wearing Moonfleece in a kingdom called Avalon where the moon is despised.

Curtis *is getting very agitated.*

Sarah *is trying to calm him.*

Zak Ahhhhh!

Link What's happening now?

Zak I'm the Queen.

Link What's happened?

Zak I've just seen Prince Jason.

Link And he's wearing Moonfleece!

Zak 'What are you wearing, my son?' 'Moonfleece.' 'Moon! Haven't you heard anything King Avalon has been saying?' 'That's crazy talk, Mum.' 'Shhh! King Avalon will hear you.' 'Too late, my love. I heard everything!' 'I'm sure he didn't mean it.' 'I do, Mum!' 'Take it off, Jason!' 'No, Avalon! I like it!' 'It's disgusting!' 'It's not!' 'Then you can't be part of this new family.' 'Please, son. Do it for me!' 'I'd do anything for you, Mum! You know I would! But I must wear Moonfleece! Moonfleece is what I am!' 'Listen, you pervert! I have ambitions! Plans for my future kingdom are taking shape. Someone like you could ruin everything for me. I can't have you around. I will you give a chest of gold to start a new life elsewhere. We will tell everyone here that you were killed in an accident. A fatal accident. I will fake all the necessary documents. You will never show your face in this kingdom again. You must never make contact with your mum. Or your younger brother.'

Link Younger brother?

Zak Prince Jason has a younger brother. Ain't I mentioned that? What a bloody oversight. His name's Prince Curtis. And Prince Curtis adores Prince Jason. You remember when their real Dad – the old King – had been killed? Prince Jason looked took care of Prince Curtis after that. And now their new Dad, this Avalon, is telling Jason he must go away and never see his Mum or Curtis again. And Jason says, 'If that's what my Mum wants, I'll do it. But only if it's what *she* wants. Do you want me to disappear, Mum? Do you?'

Curtis *is murmuring 'No . . . No . . .' now.*

His distress and agitation are becoming uncontrollable.

Others are trying to restrain and calm him.

Zak Ask me what the mum replies, Apprentice.

Slight pause.

Ask me!

Link What . . . what does Mum reply?

Zak *jumps off table and faces* **Curtis**.

Zak . . . 'Yes.'

Curtis No!

Zak Jason couldn't bear to see your mum upset again! He'd seen it after your real dad died. Jason wanted her to be happy!

Curtis I waved him off at the airport!

Zak And he went to the jungle. He sent you cards. But he came back.

Curtis I'm not listening!

Zak Avalon faked the whole thing. Documents. Human remains.

Curtis Shut up!

Zak Jason was back in this country all the time, Curtis. Travelling from place to place.

Curtis I don't believe you!

Zak I met him two years ago. In Cornwall. We lived together.

Curtis No!

Zak I was happy. But Jason wasn't. He wanted to come to you and tell you the whole story.

Curtis Then why didn't he?

Zak Because he couldn't upset your mum. He didn't want you feeling bad things about her. That's why he made me promise. No matter what happened to him. I must *never* find you. *Never* tell you the truth.

Curtis Shut up! Shut up!

Zak But now I have! And I'm glad!

Curtis Shut up!

Zak Curtis ... everything you've been told is a lie!

Curtis *launches himself at* **Zak**.

Zak *and* **Curtis** *struggle.*

Others pull **Curtis** *off.*

Curtis I don't believe it . . . Sarah? You hear what he's saying? Jason wouldn't leave me . . . My mum – she wouldn't agree . . . You *know* my mum, Sarah . . . Tom? You know her! . . . My mum wouldn't . . . my mum wouldn't . . . I *know* her . . . I know . . . I know . . . my mum . . . my mum . . . my mum . . .

Slowly, **Curtis***'s anger is spent.*

He is like a clockwork toy running down.

Slight pause.

It's almost dark outside now.

Wayne *rushes in. He is twenty-one years old and wearing a light-grey suit.*

Wayne Phew! Those stairs! . . . Dark and smelly or what, eh? Hello, everyone. Wayne. Wayne Avalon. Nice to see you all. Hello . . . Pleasure . . . Sarah! Luv! You look well. Hair's different. Suits you.

Points at **Nina**.

Wayne Library! Right? Like your dress. Green's your colour. Tom, I'm a bit out of condition, mate. I need a Tom special work-out.

Goes to **Curtis**.

Wayne Brov! What is all this? You're worrying us sick, buddy.

Stacey *rushes in. She is twenty years and wearing a light grey skirt and white blouse. She is holding* **Gavin***'s lighter.*

Stacey Oh, those stairs! Could barely see a thing! Where's that Gavin got to – Gav?!

Wayne Leave him!

Stacey But I've got his lighter.

Wayne Then he should've kept up with you! – Stace! Look who's had her hair done!

Stacey Sarah! Oh, sweetheart! You look brilliant. And that dress! You've lost weight. I hate you. Only joking. Hello, everyone . . . Pleasure . . . Hi . . . You can really feel autumn coming in now, can't you, eh?

Points at **Nina**.

Stacey Library! Right? Green's really your colour. I think it's wonderful the way you make the most of yourself.

Wayne Stace?

Indicates **Curtis**.

Stacey Oh, sweetheart. We've been worried sick.

Wayne I told him.

Stacey *goes to* **Curtis** *and holds his hand.*

Stacey You're trembling sweetheart. Wayne, he's burning up.

Wayne Let's get you home, buddy.

Wayne *heads for door.*

Stacey *tugs at* **Curtis***'s hand.*

Curtis *doesn't move.*

Stacey Oh, sweetheart. What is it?

Wayne Curt? What's up?

Stacey This block's getting gloomier by the second. Come on.

Nina He hasn't heard the end of the story.

Wayne Eh? What story's this?

Nina These two handsome boys here. They're street entertainers. They've been telling us a story.

Sarah With three things in.

Nina Things we chose.

Stacey Oh, how cute!

Sarah So far we've only had two of the three things.

Tommy That's right, yeah.

Nina I'm sure when we've heard the whole story all of us will want to go.

Stacey Oh, you *must* hear the end, Curt. Of course you must. It'll drive you crazy if you don't. Remember when your mum recorded that murder mystery for us, Wayne? And we sat up late one night to watch it? And just as we were about to find out who done it the screen went all fuzzy and the snooker came on. Ooo, we could've killed your mum, couldn't we? Joke.

Wayne Do you mind if we listen on?

Stacey Oh, I'm sure they wouldn't.

Nina The more the merrier.

Wayne That's great. Thank you.

Stacey Yes, thank you.

Slight pause.

Link O Storyteller . . .

Stacey Ooo! Goose bumps. Look!

Link One thing remains to be woven into the fabric of your tale. Please put us out of our misery and tell us . . .

Slight pause.

Zak *goes to speak but can't.*

He shakes his head.

Wayne Something wrong?

Nina Sore throat.

Stacey You need a good gargle with lemon juice and honey. You put it in hot water as hot as you can bare and –

Makes gargling noise.

Slight pause.

Link I think ... *I* can finish it.

Nina *You* know the end?

Link I ... I think I do, yeah. Zak? It's the mate you told me about, ain't it?

Zak *nods.*

Nina Go on, then, brave Apprentice.

Moonlight is now filling the room.

Link The Prince ... he travels for many years. Until he reaches a place where land ends and sea begins. The Prince sits on the beach and thinks of his old kingdom. He misses it so much but knows he can never go back. He made a promise to the Queen – is this right, Zak?

Zak *nods.*

Link He made a promise to the Queen and the Prince would never do anything to upset the Queen. He saw the Queen very upset once before, you see. And he couldn't bear to see her like that again.

Stacey Question! Why can't he go back exactly?

Link The Prince loves moonlight.

Nina And moonlight has been banished from the kingdom.

Wayne How can you banish moonlight?

Stacey It's a fairy tale, silly.

Link And then the Prince sees dolphins swimming out in the ocean. They seem to be calling his name. The Prince walks into the water. The dolphins call him further and further out. The Prince swims until he can swim no more. He floats on his back and looks up at the sky. The moon is full and very bright.

Slight pause.

Stacey So . . . the Prince kills himself. Is that it?

Link Yeah.

Wayne And that's . . . the end?

Nina Yes.

Stacey Well, I don't think you'll have Walt Disney knocking at your door for that one. But very good, though. Very entertaining. Weren't it, Wayne?

Wayne Yeah, very.

Sarah When did this happen? I mean . . . what time of year?

Zak The middle of summer.

Sarah Like the summer . . . just gone?

Zak Yes.

Nina Does the Queen know of the Prince's death?

Zak Not yet she doesn't.

Picks up his bags.

Link *finishes packing the last few things.*

Zak *and* **Link** *head for door.*

Curtis Zak?

Zak *looks at* **Curtis**.

Slight pause.

Zak *goes over to* **Curtis**.

Slight pause.

Zak *strokes* **Curtis***'s cheek.*

Curtis *reaches out and touches the jacket.*

Slight pause.

Stacey Wayne?

Wayne Don't panic.

Zak *and* **Link** *leave.*

Nina Time to go, my dearies – Alex! Your muscles up to it, big boy?

Alex Yeah.

Nina (*at* **Tommy**) What about you, Ocean Spray?

Tommy *looks at* **Curtis**.

Curtis *nods.*

Tommy A pleasure.

Nina Ooo! I feel a dance coming on.

Alex *and* **Tommy** *pick* **Nina** *up.*

Those with torches are turning them on.

Jez (*at* **Curtis**) Bye.

Curtis *stares.*

Alex Sarah?

Sarah . . . Yeah.

Nina, **Alex**, **Tommy**, *followed by* **Jez**, *leave.*

Sarah *looks at* **Curtis**.

Slight pause.

Gavin *rushes in, breathless, holding his eye.*

Gavin That . . . that bloke hit me!

Wayne What bloke?

Gavin In the gay-boy jacket – Oww! It's swelling!

Wayne Help show the others out. It's dark.

Gavin But I've only just got up here. I'm all out of puff.

Wayne Well, you should quit bloody smoking, then, shouldn't you!

Gavin But –

Wayne *growls at* **Gavin**.

Gavin *runs out.*

Stacey Don't be a stranger, Sarah. Wayne's mum's always asking after you. Ain't she, Wayne?

Wayne Always.

Sarah *leaves.*

Stacey Oh, Curtis, my lovely, what's all this about?

Wayne I think I know. It's that bloke.

Stacey What one?

Wayne The one in the jacket. He reminded you of your dead brother, didn't he?

Stacey Oh, sweetheart! We thought you were all over that.

Wayne We all lose people, buddy. You can't grieve all your life.

Stacey It was awful what happened to Jason, sweetheart. I never had the pleasure of meeting him but, from what I hear, he was a charming person with everything before him. But sometimes, you know, things happen for a reason. We don't know the reason. Only God knows that. Right, Wayne?

Wayne Right, Stace.

Stacey It's like when my sausage dog died. I loved that sausage dog. Banger its name was. And one day I looked in its little basket and Banger was as stiff as a board. I cried and cried. Dad wasn't much help. He said we should use it as a draught excluder. I got no sympathy at all. Dad wouldn't let me even bury Banger in the back garden. So I wrapped Banger in some kitchen foil and took him over to the park. They had a flower garden there and I thought it would be nice to bury Banger amongst all those daffodils.

So I dug a hole and put little Banger in. I was just covering Banger up with earth when I heard the park keeper yelling at me. Oh, the names he called me. The language. I ran and ran. He chased me. I ran all the way to the market. I was gasping. I went into this corner shop to get a can of something. I took something out the cooler and opened it and swigged a mouthful. Ooo, it was delicious. It really was. I put my hand in my pocket and – no money! Not a penny! I glanced up at this lovely Pakistani gentleman behind the counter. But he was serving someone else. So I thought, I'll pop home and get the money and then I'll come back and pay him. I'd only taken one step out the bloody door when the lovely Pakistani gentleman rushes over and grabs me arm and accuses me of stealing. Me! Well, I start screaming and shouting and giving the lovely Pakistani gentleman a piece of my mind. And that's when this man comes out the shop next door. A white man! The man pays the lovely Pakistani gentleman the money I owe him and takes me into his own shop. And who's answering the phone? Wayne. Cos the man who paid for my drink was none other than Mr Avalon. So you see, sweetheart, if it weren't for my dead Banger I'd never have met Wayne.

Sarah *appears in doorway, holding a lit torch and a packet of photos.*

Sarah Oh. Sorry. I've ... got something for Curtis.

Indicating photos.

Stacey We're just on our way home, sweetheart. You wanna come back with us and – ?

Sarah I don't think so, Stacey.

Slight pause.

Curtis I'm staying here a bit longer.

Wayne Not a good idea, buddy.

Curtis I'm not bloody going yet!

Slight pause.

Stacey Let him have a last look round, Wayne. Get it out of his system.

Wayne We're on the brink of a great political victory, buddy.

Stacey We've all worked so hard for it.

Wayne You more than anyone. You know that.

Stacey We don't want anything to rock the boat, sweetheart.

Wayne Nothing *can* rock the boat. So long as people behave themselves.

Wayne *and* **Stacey** *head for door.*

At the door, **Wayne** *stops and looks back at* **Curtis**.

Wayne You know, buddy, sometimes we hear rumours about stuff and it . . . well, it confuses us. We wonder what's true, what's not true. It's happened to me. I've heard little whispers late at night. Did this happen? Did that happen? But you know what I do? I ask Dad. After all, he's there to look out for me, ain't he. So I ask Dad and whatever he tells me . . . that's the truth. Life's simpler that way.

Stacey Wayne's dad loves you, Curt.

Wayne He's *our* dad. And, yes, he *does* love you. We *all* love you. Love you very much. You know that. Don't you, bruv?

Curt . . . Yes. I know.

Wayne *and* **Stacey** *walk out.*

Slight pause.

Sarah Zak wanted me to give you these.

Curtis What are they?

Sarah Photos. Taken of someone on a beach. Earlier this year.

Curtis Have you . . . ?

Sarah No.

Puts photos on table.

All those times we said, 'I wonder what Jason would've thought.' Remember? When I decided art school is what I'm going to aim for. And now – when the leaves are turning brown. He loved this time of year, didn't he? And remember how we said how pleased he would've been when you . . . you and me . . .

Gently weeps.

Curtis *steps towards her.*

Sarah No!

Curtis *stops.*

Slight pause.

Sarah I don't feel young at all. Do you? I feel like I've lived a million years and . . . and gone through hundreds of wars and I can't tell anyone about them cos when they look at me all they see is this . . . young face. But it's not the face I should have. It's not my face.

Sarah *goes to leave –*

Curtis Sarah.

Sarah *stops and looks at* **Curtis**.

Sarah What?

Slight pause.

What do you wanna say, Curtis?

Slight pause.

What do you want to do?

Curtis *doesn't move.*

Slight pause.

Sarah *leaves.*

Curtis *looks at the photos on the table.*

Slight pause.

Curtis *approaches table.*

Slight pause.

Curtis *picks photos up.*

Slight pause.

Curtis *opens packet of photos.*

He hesitates before looking at them.

Curtis *looks at first photo.*

The dogs start barking.

Curtis *continues looking at photos.*

The dogs bark louder and louder.

The dogs bark louder and louder.

Blackout.

Methuen Drama Student Editions

Jean Anouilh *Antigone* • John Arden *Serjeant Musgrave's Dance* Alan Ayckbourn *Confusions* • Aphra Behn *The Rover* • Edward Bond *Lear* • *Saved* • Bertolt Brecht *The Caucasian Chalk Circle* • *Fear and Misery in the Third Reich* • *The Good Person of Szechwan* • *Life of Galileo* • *Mother Courage and her Children*• *The Resistible Rise of Arturo Ui* • *The Threepenny Opera* • Anton Chekhov *The Cherry Orchard* • *The Seagull* • *Three Sisters* • *Uncle Vanya* • Caryl Churchill *Serious Money* • *Top Girls* • Shelagh Delaney *A Taste of Honey* • Euripides *Elektra* • *Medea*• Dario Fo *Accidental Death of an Anarchist* • Michael Frayn *Copenhagen* • John Galsworthy *Strife* • Nikolai Gogol *The Government Inspector* • Robert Holman *Across Oka* • Henrik Ibsen *A Doll's House* • *Ghosts*• *Hedda Gabler* • Charlotte Keatley *My Mother Said I Never Should* • Bernard Kops *Dreams of Anne Frank* • Federico García Lorca *Blood Wedding* • *Doña Rosita the Spinster* (bilingual edition) •*The House of Bernarda Alba* • (bilingual edition) • *Yerma* (bilingual edition) • David Mamet *Glengarry Glen Ross* • *Oleanna* • Patrick Marber *Closer* • John Marston *Malcontent* • Martin McDonagh *The Lieutenant of Inishmore* • Joe Orton *Loot* • Luigi Pirandello *Six Characters in Search of an Author* • Mark Ravenhill *Shopping and F***ing* • Willy Russell *Blood Brothers* • *Educating Rita* • Sophocles *Antigone* • *Oedipus the King* • Wole Soyinka *Death and the King's Horseman* • Shelagh Stephenson *The Memory of Water* • August Strindberg *Miss Julie* • J. M. Synge *The Playboy of the Western World* • Theatre Workshop *Oh What a Lovely War* Timberlake Wertenbaker *Our Country's Good* • Arnold Wesker *The Merchant* • Oscar Wilde *The Importance of Being Earnest* • Tennessee Williams *A Streetcar Named Desire* • *The Glass Menagerie*

Methuen Drama Modern Plays

include work by

Edward Albee
Jean Anouilh
John Arden
Margaretta D'Arcy
Peter Barnes
Sebastian Barry
Brendan Behan
Dermot Bolger
Edward Bond
Bertolt Brecht
Howard Brenton
Anthony Burgess
Simon Burke
Jim Cartwright
Caryl Churchill
Complicite
Noël Coward
Lucinda Coxon
Sarah Daniels
Nick Darke
Nick Dear
Shelagh Delaney
David Edgar
David Eldridge
Dario Fo
Michael Frayn
John Godber
Paul Godfrey
David Greig
John Guare
Peter Handke
David Harrower
Jonathan Harvey
Iain Heggie
Declan Hughes
Terry Johnson
Sarah Kane
Charlotte Keatley
Barrie Keeffe
Howard Korder
Robert Lepage
Doug Lucie
Martin McDonagh
John McGrath
Terrence McNally
David Mamet
Patrick Marber
Arthur Miller
Mtwa, Ngema & Simon
Tom Murphy
Phyllis Nagy
Peter Nichols
Sean O'Brien
Joseph O'Connor
Joe Orton
Louise Page
Joe Penhall
Luigi Pirandello
Stephen Poliakoff
Franca Rame
Mark Ravenhill
Philip Ridley
Reginald Rose
Willy Russell
Jean-Paul Sartre
Sam Shepard
Wole Soyinka
Simon Stephens
Shelagh Stephenson
Peter Straughan
C. P. Taylor
Theatre Workshop
Sue Townsend
Judy Upton
Timberlake Wertenbaker
Roy Williams
Snoo Wilson
Victoria Wood

Methuen Drama Contemporary Dramatists
include

John Arden (two volumes)
Arden & D'Arcy
Peter Barnes (three volumes)
Sebastian Barry
Dermot Bolger
Edward Bond (eight volumes)
Howard Brenton
(two volumes)
Richard Cameron
Jim Cartwright
Caryl Churchill (two volumes)
Sarah Daniels (two volumes)
Nick Darke
David Edgar (three volumes)
David Eldridge
Ben Elton
Dario Fo (two volumes)
Michael Frayn (three volumes)
David Greig
John Godber (four volumes)
Paul Godfrey
John Guare
Lee Hall (two volumes)
Peter Handke
Jonathan Harvey
(two volumes)
Declan Hughes
Terry Johnson (three volumes)
Sarah Kane
Barrie Keeffe
Bernard-Marie Koltès
(two volumes)
Franz Xaver Kroetz
David Lan
Bryony Lavery
Deborah Levy
Doug Lucie
David Mamet (four volumes)
Martin McDonagh
Duncan McLean
Anthony Minghella
(two volumes)
Tom Murphy (six volumes)
Phyllis Nagy
Anthony Neilsen (two volumes)
Philip Osment
Gary Owen
Louise Page
Stewart Parker (two volumes)
Joe Penhall (two volumes)
Stephen Poliakoff
(three volumes)
David Rabe (two volumes)
Mark Ravenhill (two volumes)
Christina Reid
Philip Ridley
Willy Russell
Eric-Emmanuel Schmitt
Ntozake Shange
Sam Shepard (two volumes)
Wole Soyinka (two volumes)
Simon Stephens (two volumes)
Shelagh Stephenson
David Storey (three volumes)
Sue Townsend
Judy Upton
Michel Vinaver
(two volumes)
Arnold Wesker (two volumes)
Michael Wilcox
Roy Williams (three volumes)
Snoo Wilson (two volumes)
David Wood (two volumes)
Victoria Wood

Methuen Drama Classical Greek Dramatists

Aeschylus Plays: One
(Persians, Seven Against Thebes, Suppliants, Prometheus Bound)

Aeschylus Plays: Two
(Oresteia: Agamemnon, Libation-Bearers, Eumenides)

Aristophanes Plays: One
(Acharnians, Knights, Peace, Lysistrata)

Aristophanes Plays: Two
(Wasps, Clouds, Birds, Festival Time, Frogs)

Aristophanes & Menander: New Comedy
(Women in Power, Wealth, The Malcontent, The Woman from Samos)

Euripides Plays: One
(Medea, The Phoenician Women, Bacchae)

Euripides Plays: Two
(Hecuba, The Women of Troy, Iphigeneia at Aulis, Cyclops)

Euripides Plays: Three
(Alkestis, Helen, Ion)

Euripides Plays: Four
(Elektra, Orestes, Iphigeneia in Tauris)

Euripides Plays: Five
(Andromache, Herakles' Children, Herakles)

Euripides Plays: Six
(Hippolytos, Suppliants, Rhesos)

Sophocles Plays: One
(Oedipus the King, Oedipus at Colonus, Antigone)

Sophocles Plays: Two
(Ajax, Women of Trachis, Electra, Philoctetes)